DON JUAN
and the Art of
SEXUAL ENERGY

By the same author:

Medicine Dream

DON JUAN
and the Art of
SEXUAL ENERGY

*The Rainbow Serpent
of the Toltecs*

MERILYN TUNNESHENDE

Bear & Company
Rochester, Vermont

Bear & Company
One Park Street
Rochester, Vermont 05767
www.InnerTraditions.com

Library of Congress Cataloging-in-Publication Data
Tunneshende, Merilyn.
    Don Juan and the art of sexual energy : the rainbow serpent of the Toltecs / Merilyn Tunneshende.
        p. cm.
Rev. ed. of: Rainbow serpent.
ISBN 1-879181-63-0 (alk. Paper)
    1. Tunneshende, Merilyn. 2. Sex—Miscellanea. 3. Shamanism—Mexico—Miscellanea. I. Tunneshende, Merilyn. Rainbow serpent. II. Title.
    BF1623.S4 T86 2001
    299'.93—dc21

                                                            2001018441

Printed and bound in Canada

10   9   8   7   6   5   4   3   2   1

This book was typeset in Sabon with Bell Gothic and Schneidler Initials as the display typefaces.

To "Goyacle," Geronimo, a great Chiricahua warrior

CONTENTS

Preface   ix

Introduction   xi

1. Dream Bridging   1

2. Making Peace with the Angry Mother–Father   13

3. Recapitulation   23

4. Exploring Celibacy   33

5. Retrieving Our Lost Energy   43

6. Drawing and Releasing Energy in Nature   54

7. Shapeshifter Dreaming   63

8. Masculine and Feminine Polarity   72

9. Cultivating the Sexual Energy   83

10. Sisterhood and Brotherhood   95

11. Dreaming the Body   104

12. Energy Healing   115

13. The Female Orgasmic Practices   128

14. The Male Sexual Energy   140

15. The Celestial Wash   149

16. The Phallic Female   157

17. Life-Force Energy Dance   165

18. Sacred Union   172

19. The Unicorn   178

20. Non-Earthly Realms of Energy   187

21. The Death Defier   195

22. The Eagle   203

23. The Fire Within   211

Epilogue   218

PREFACE

HOW TO APPROACH THE PRACTICES
PRESENTED IN THIS BOOK

IN EUROPE, WHERE THIS BOOK WAS FIRST RELEASED, PEOPLE have responded to its simplicity and have asked me if it is deliberate. I tell them yes. My mentors and I feel that simplicity is required because we are but children when sexual energy begins to complicate our lives. In fact, from the moment of our conception, sexual energy plays a vital role as one of the major forces that will shape our lives.

Gentleness, simplicity, and humor are the required medicine, sharing just enough at first, and not too much, so as not to frighten, overload, or confound and so as to allow the natural cleansing and liberating process to begin. A friend of mine called Alfonsina said that she thought this book should be written to resemble "lessons for big children." She said there is an inherent kindness in even the most terrifying children's stories that is very beneficial to the body. I couldn't agree with her more.

And so, following that advice, I have endeavored to share the kindness and humor in all of this sexual energy work, in addition to some specific practices. As to the practices themselves, take them slowly. Don't be in a rush to fabricate an experience. Take one practice at a time. Work with it consistently and gently until it begins to produce beneficial effects in the body. Don't be greedy to "get it all" and race through to arrive at the last practice. There is so much more! What I offer here is simply a beginning that will put your feet on the right road.

Some of the practices are more advanced than others. Some are quite advanced indeed. These will always reference an earlier practice, which one needs to experience successfully before moving on the the next level. All of the work, even that which seems the most simple, will produce profound results. So again, there is no need to rush. This is not a competition.

With that in mind, my last bit of advice is to enjoy! Joy is a quality we have all but lost and it is very good medicine to rediscover it. The practices do flow in a natural order, so simply trust the process. There is no need to skip around. Try to maintain a relaxed focus and healthy, loving, enthusiastic curiosity as you embark on this spiritual journey.

INTRODUCTION

IN 1979 WHILE JOURNEYING TO MEXICO, I MET AN OLD
native gentleman in the desert of Arizona who was
forever to change my life. He was a solitary figure, a Yuma, or
Kw'tsan as they like to be called, and was notorious for a very
potent and mysterious shamanic ability called Dream Power.
This Nagual (Shapeshifter Shaman) was commonly known by
the Spanish pen name of don Juan Matus. Over the years that
I knew him, he endeavored to teach me his special form of
dreaming and share its potency with me. I discovered under
his tutelage and benevolence that Dream Power is an indis-
pensable tool in healing that literally makes miracles happen.
I also came to realize that Dream Power has strong links to
our sexual energy and to the development of our energy bodies, which, although it shouldn't have, came as quite a surprise to me.

As we continued our association, my own Dream Power
grew and I began to acquire full-fledged entry into don
Juan's world. It was at this time that he revealed to me that
he had "seen" we were the same sort, energetic counterparts.
As I matured as a woman, my feelings toward him changed
from awe to something more like love. If I truly examine my

perceptions and feelings, though, I realize that I loved him on first sight, despite the differences in our ages and cultures.

In 1994 my mentor and energetic counterpart leapt from this world by literally walking out of his body, experiencing the Fire Within and Rainbow Crossing of the Spirit Waters at death. These are the classic teachings of the Rainbow Serpent, a body of transformational sexual energy wisdom found within the culture of the Toltec-Maya. Having been joined with don Juan in a sacred union of energies before, after, and at the time he left this world, I found myself the inheritor of his magical realms and of his desert homeland. One among several still-living members of this legacy is a powerful sorceress by the name of doña Celestina de la Soledad. Another is the artful Dreamer and healer Chon Yakil, once pen-named don Genaro by Carlos Castaneda.

At first glance, doña Celestina appears to be a full-blooded witch. There is no doubt about it and no other way to put it. The Doña, now eighty-four years of age, was sixty-six at the time of our first meeting in 1981. She stands a powerful 5'7", my exact height, has a Native face with gray hair, which she pulls up into a head rag turban, and fully lives up to her given name "Soledad"—Solitude. She always wears a simple black dress to cover her dark, lean, muscular body and scarcely ever smiles, but has long, beautiful teeth. It was doña Celestina, terror upon terror, who took charge of my instruction in the ways of female power.

I will never forget the day don Juan took me across the Mexican border into San Luis Rio Colorado to meet her. Doña Celestina was standing on a street corner in her black dress and sandals, whacking the stalks from large ears of corn with a massive machete, partially husking the ears with forceful strokes and tossing them into a metal washtub of boiling water which sat upon coals smoldering on an old oil drum. She leered at me while she worked and her dark shadow leapt in my direction, stretching over the sunlit curb at a diagonal. It hovered where I stood. This is no healer, no medicine woman, I thought to myself, chilled. She is a bona fide witch, through and through. Don Juan stared at me fiercely, reading my thoughts. "This is your teacher," he said, and made the appropriate introductions.

Doña Celestina is a composite of Corn Mother and Dragon Lady. I found her to be as fierce and as capable as they come. Among her areas of energetic expertise are longevity wisdom, sexual energy practices, and powerful antidote witchcraft. During my continued stays in her home in San Luis Rio Colorado, Sonora, I worked daily to earn my keep, and still do when I visit. She tolerates nothing less. In the beginning of the relationship I scrubbed the tile walls, counters, and floors with a boar bristle brush until they glistened, and washed clothing spotless by hand. Later I graduated to ironing the clothing over and over until the creases were as sharp and straight as blades, and then mopped the tiles until you could eat off the floors. Finally, having mastered the aforementioned tasks, I joined a small rank of girls she taught to machine sew straight seams at a lightning pace. Together we would finish piles of clothes for later sale in the market, all following her expert example and under her witchly scrutiny. It never once occurred to any of us to think to herself "this is an apprenticeship?" It was a matter of survival.

At night, when the shadows crept and the younger girls went home or to bed, doña Celestina and I always went into her dark workroom to learn "trabajitos" (little jobs). This was her altar room for séance, counseling, and hex anti-hex. It was forbidden to enter unless she was accompanying, and no one would have ever dared break that rule. At the first hint of twilight, we'd dine in the old tiled kitchen on simple but powerful fare—corn, squash, beans, chilies, and tortillas usually, followed by strong coffee. We'd leave the dishes to soak, and enjoy the change in light and breeze from bentwood rockers on her inner patio. And then at dark, like two drifting shadows, we'd enter the smoky altar room and sit across from one another at her rustic worktable. The large room was then and is still now always lit only by candlelight, and every conceivable energy can be found within it.

We often discussed and worked well into the night. Many of the things I have learned from doña Celestina are terrifying, but she teaches by nature what she has to do to survive, much like the deposed Mother Earth in a time of earth changes. At the core of her teachings lies a body of spiritualized sexual energy practices and longevity wisdom. These are the areas I shall focus upon in this account.

With this centerpiece, I also share more of the sexual energy and dreaming practices taught to me by my other two mentors, don Juan Matus and Chon Yakil. For them, there is a profound connection between sexual energy and dreaming, especially shamanic dreaming. Some initiations into the shamanic realms of don Juan Matus and Chon Yakil have been explored at length in my first book, *Medicine Dream, A Nagual Woman's Energetic Healing*, which recounts how I, an educator, was thrust into the world of shamanic healing rituals and dream "double" development. The introduction of doña Celestina and her perspectives is completely new within the domain of this current book.

The present focus of my work in this area, with Chon Yakil, an eighty-six-year-old practitioner of the Toltec-Mayan branch of Nagualism, has now evolved. At Chon's request I have been acting as his ambassador to the medical community, appearing with psychiatrists and physicians on numerous panels about shamanism, alternative medicine, and traditional Western medicine. In detailing the actual Dreaming practices prescribed for healing, based on seeing energy directly, I am able to demonstrate that illness and other maladies have spiritual and energetic precursors that complement their physical manifestations.

All of this knowledge, combined with what I have learned from don Juan of the true and authentic Fire Within energetic crossing practice undertaken at the moment of death, comprises newly discovered aspects of ancient Nagualist shamanism and contains valuable missing pieces of the world's shamanic, spiritual, and metaphysical puzzle. I have found that, in addition to the Toltec, the Nahua, and the Maya, many other indigenous cultures have had the Nagual, the Shapeshifter Sun or Fire Being (Uay Kin in the Mayan language) and may have once had knowledge of the Fire Within. The Q'ero, descendants of the Inka, are one such example. The Yaqui, Yuma, and Dineh, as well as early Mississippian cultures, are yet others. Nagualism has been found to have its roots in the same knowledge pool that fed the pre-Tibetan and Siberian shamanic traditions, and these began long before, and occurred during, the transcontinental shamanic sweep, perhaps 40,000 years ago.

Knowledge of the Rainbow Serpent fire is found in pieces within the tradition of Kundalini Yoga, in the Tibetan development of the Rainbow Body, within Taoism as the immortal body, and among the Sioux and other native peoples as the Spirits of the Rainbow World. The Australian aboriginals refer openly to the Rainbow Serpent as the primordial life energy and have many ancient rock paintings representing the energy.

In this new book I am sharing what I have witnessed and experienced of these ancient ways, the lessons taught to me and how I have seen people benefit from dramatic healing, energy, and expanded, enlightening awareness. Many of the teachings are newly revealed and seem to have been withheld until the appropriate moment. Now the feeling is that it is time.

Humankind, the Earth, and all of her creatures are currently facing an impending evolutionary shift and an opportunity for realignment with our best possible intent. Much of what is missing in the current worldview is to be found within ancient wisdom traditions. Simply put, the paradigm shifts in perception and energy that are now being shared, have the capacity to heal and to be practical tools that we can use to survive, to evolve, and to aspire toward enlightenment.

Blessed be.

Dream Bridging

IN 1993 I MOVED BACK TO YUMA, ARIZONA. IT WAS TO be the last year I would spend with all three of my mentors in their physical bodies. The drive had been a long one, four days across the southern United States in my white Jeep Cherokee, marking the distances. I was tired of sitting with my foot to the gas pedal, but when I saw the Picacho Peak, one of the first distinguishable features of the Yuman horizon, I felt a surge of energy and exhilaration.

I arrived in Old Town and went straight to Lute's Casino, which is not really a casino at all, but rather a turn-of-the-century pool hall, saloon, and domino parlor that exists as if within a mythical oasis in time. There I was told by some Yuma Indians, who live across the Colorado River on the reservation, that don Juan had relocated and was now living in the Cocopa Mountains south of Mexicali.

After all my driving, somehow this did not surprise me much. I knew how he liked to roam the desert, but it meant more time in the jeep, for which I now felt mysteriously prepared. I got directions to the mountains and the town and then went to settle my things into a small adobe apartment don Juan had found for me in Old Town, near the reservation. The apartment was the kind of place that looks so simple, warm and empty you don't want to put anything into it. It was private and flooded by light on smooth walls and floors, with desert vegetation surrounding it and an irrigation canal behind it. By the time I unloaded and showered, it was late afternoon. I sat back in the driver's seat and headed southwest toward Baja California.

The drive, as it often is in the Yuman desert, was beautiful. First riding under the sunny, cloudless sky past the Algodones sand dunes used in many Hollywood films to simulate the Sahara desert, then turning south onto the craggy Baja peninsula and heading for the blackened lava peaks, now burnished golden by the setting sun. I arrived in the little Cocopa town of Pozo, on the Mexican Baja Peninsula, shortly after the sun descended behind those peaks. There was nothing much to it, just a couple of dirt roads with small cement or wattle-and-daub houses, and the backdrop of the mountains. I found a friend of don Juan's, Luis Tanfoya, sitting on a wooden chair in the shadowy front area outside of his tiny cement home. Getting out of my jeep, I greeted him politely and asked directions. With his toothless grin shining, he offered me a cup of water and pointed up the dirt road to a small pinkish home at the end of it.

After savoring the cup of cool water and chatting casually, I drove to the last house on the right side of the road. Large yucca were growing out front and to the back, there were several huge cardon cacti that attain massive height and live for several hundred years. "Don Juan?" I called as I pulled a small cooler filled with several packages of smoked rainbow trout out of the passenger side of my jeep.

"Presente," he called back in Spanish from the back yard.

I went eagerly around back without entering the house. He was dressed in a black shirt and slacks, sitting on a wooden chair peeling pitayas—colorfully festive cactus fruits about the size of light bulbs—with a small hunting knife. He put down the clay bowl of shavings and stood up to greet me with a big hug.

"This is for you," I said, referring to the cooler, which I dropped to the ground with the force of his squeeze.

"Sit down," he invited, pulling another wooden chair out of the back room of the house. "Mmmm!" He snooped in the cooler and then, closing it, offered me a clay bowl filled with peeled pitayas.

The luscious fruits were dazzling white, green, orange, red, scarlet and blackish purple. I felt I had never seen such vibrant fruits. I selected the dark purple one and bit into it. The rich meat was juicy and a bit fibrous; the juice, almost an elixir filled with little black seeds. I slurped and wiped the purple stain from my mouth and fingers with a moist cloth that don Juan handed me from the bare wooden table where he had set his knife, the peelings, and the rest of the unpeeled pitayas.

The sky was now shades of crimson and a small flock of grackles started cackling from a mesquite tree nearby. "I admire your restraint in not asking me what I am doing even further out in the middle of nowhere," don Juan joked.

"There is a saying among the Arabs that God created the desert so that he could be by himself," I responded in kind.

Don Juan laughed heartily. "This is an *ejido*. Do you know that word in Spanish?"

"Like a rancheria, or a tribal or communal egalitarian farm?" I asked, searching my mind for a proper translation.

Don Juan smirked at my lengthy definition. "Yes. This is the style in which most of the desert river cultures, from the Mohave to the Yaqui, used to live. To be a part of the community one must work, so I am here as the local Kwaxot."

"The shaman with Dream Power," I attempted to translate from Yuma.

"Right! Of course our homes were different, made of desert materials, but this is the influence of the government."

He patted the pink cement wall of the little house he had been given by the Cocopa community. "Precisely why I moved from Yuma for a time. Too much government interference with the Indians. In desperation, they are considering a casino, right across from the reservation bridge. I hope they build it, if that's what it takes to get a fair shake from Uncle Sam."

I pondered the possibility of a casino on Yuma land. "Being Yuma you can live on either side of the border, then?"

"I can visit tribal members here for an 'indefinite' time," he grinned slyly. "As a Yuma Indian I can cross the border without papers. Don't you remember that I taught you to do the same, to cross the border without papers?"

"Of course, yes I do! By saying that I am a U.S. resident of whatever American border town I happen to be near, who has only been across for the day shopping." I laughed out loud. "I always thought that was some of your sorcery. I still use that trick. It has given me so much pleasure to hypnotize the government's consumer mentality with the phrase, 'I was shopping!' It works even if I have been in Mexico for months, as long as I don't have excessive baggage."

"A metaphor for life," don Juan reflected humorously and somewhat dramatically. "Not only has it given you pleasure, it has also given you a taste of freedom, a beautiful fruit waiting only to be picked." He reached across the table so that he might offer me another exquisitely peeled pitaya from the bowl.

As I pondered his gesture he added, "Your timing couldn't be better. I'm overjoyed to see you, and also very glad that I won't have to hitch a ride to San Luis! I have some business there tomorrow."

Just beginning to recover from four-and-a-half days in my jeep, I thought of the three-hour drive awaiting us in the morning. "As a matter of fact, you have some business there as well," don Juan hinted and then went silent.

"What kind of business?" I asked.

It was almost dark. Don Juan rose and motioned for me to follow him inside. He lit a kerosene lamp and I saw that the back room was a kitchen, furnished with a small gas stove, several large freestanding water jars with lids, a sink, and a wooden table and chairs. "This place has cold-water plumbing thanks to the Mexican campaign for potable water in small villages. Don't drink it, though," he laughed.

"What business?" I repeated.

He continued walking into the main room, holding the kerosene lamp. There were thick straw mats on the floor and hand-woven blankets folded against one wall. The lantern light cast eerie shadows filled with golden hues against the open front window donned with purple twilight and the silhouette of one large yucca. I yawned. Don Juan motioned me to sit on a mat near the window. He seated himself on a mat next to me.

"What business do I have in San Luis, besides accompanying you tomorrow?" I insisted sleepily.

"I can't tell you yet. You Dream your way there tonight and discover the reason for yourself. You won't have any trouble. You're already falling asleep, aren't you?"

I confessed that the long drive had finally caught up with me and taken its toll. "It's not the drive," he laughed softly. "There is magnificent energy on the move. See if you can glimpse it tonight in Dreaming and tomorrow we'll try to bridge into the Dream." He didn't need to say more. I was already dozing on the mat. Don Juan passed me a blanket and I fell asleep the minute I covered my body.

My Dreaming opened as if riding an elevator up into my luminous energy body. A sliding door then appeared, parted, and I found myself in the sunlit patio of doña Celestina de la Soledad's home in San Luis. I became hyperalert, not only because I was Dreaming lucidly, but because doña Celestina is a powerful Cocopa sorceress and I did not want her to sense my presence in her home.

There was beautiful iridescent beadwork on a clear glass table. Someone seemed to be beading a snake out of sheer rainbows. I sensed Chon's presence and heard his laughter in the distance. Since Chon is a Maya healer and lives in the Yucatan region of Mexico, far from where I was at that moment in don Juan's home, it seemed odd to hear him. A golden cauldron was steaming near a lush papaya tree and a fragrance, alternately jasmine, then heliotrope, hung in the air. Beautiful sphere-like music wafted intermittently with the fragrance. Long slender green stalks in bloom with swirling pearlescent cone-shaped blossoms pointed upwards in the flower garden near the entrance to the house. A fountain splashed a tube of water, silvery translucent, liquid mother of pearl.

I heard don Juan's voice tell me to "open this Dream" and I sat down, humming, and rocked in a bent willow rocker.

I awoke in the morning replenished and humming the same tune. The sun was barely up and the air was fresh. Don Juan was already up fixing eggs with *machaca*, a dried beef prepared in Sonora. There is no mistaking the wonderful smell of machaca and giant Sonoran tortillas, so thin they are translucent and larger than serving platters.

I went down the hall off the main room and found the promised indoor plumbing: a toilet, a sink attached to the wall, and a shower spigot with no curtain, just the small tile floor with a drain in the center. By the time I was showered and changed, breakfast was almost on the table and coffee was brewing. I hummed the mysterious tune of my night's Dreaming as I dried my short hair. Two Gambel quails then called back to me from a cactus that I could see in the morning light through the small bathroom window. With hungry anticipation I headed for the kitchen.

"Buenas dias!" don Juan greeted me cheerfully, setting a steaming plate on the rustic table. He was grinning, as he often did after following my Dreaming with his own. I seated myself and he poured me a mug of hot coffee. "We can talk about Dreaming during the entire drive to San Luis, if you wish. For now, let's eat so that we can be on our way. Someone will be expecting us," he said mysteriously.

I ate the delicious breakfast of hot salty meat, eggs and tortillas with considerable enthusiasm. Don Juan smiled, watching me eat with apparent interest. "I'm glad to see that you are enjoying food and have gained a little weight. I don't care what your women's magazines say, skinny women are unhealthy. Up until now you have always had a tendency to be too thin. Now you look robust, muscular and strong." He got up from the table to clear our plates. After helping him, I repacked my jeep and within thirty minutes we were driving up the dirt road out of Pozo.

Once we were off the rough roads and on the highway, don Juan began a discussion of Dreaming. He relaxed in the front seat as if to prepare for a long talk. "Every power in our culture is derived from Dream Power," he began. "Dreaming is the deepest natural and healthy trance that the body induces. It is because of this depth and its visionary capacity, and also due to the fact that the energy body may journey fully, that Dreaming is the most highly regarded among trance states.

"One may truly enter into sacred space and time, go through gateways, act, and bring back powers. The key, as you know, is lucidity, a key which most members of the white culture have lost, but which we, the native peoples of the Colorado River area, never threw away. What you were doing last night is called bridging, for lack of a better word in English. One enters into Dreaming with lucidity, and then seeks to Dream something that one may open, bring back and step into in the waking time.

"This is how healers find their medicine plants and songs, how war leaders are imbued with power, and public leaders learn what to say to the people. In order for the Dreaming to truly have power, it must be brought into the world for all to see. Throughout the Baja here and up the Colorado River towards Nevada, there are canyons and caves filled with murals which embody, or bring back a shaman's visions. In seeing these, one enters into the power of the Dreams. They are recorded for all who are initiated into their use.

"It is not required, however, to paint the Dream into the magical womb space of a cave or canyon. A powerful shaman may carry his or her womb space bodily and energetically and may open it and step into it whenever it is necessary. This manifests the Dreaming. What we will be Seeing today is how well you are able to carry your Dreaming in your womb, and whether or not you are able to fully step into it."

I got the gist of his explanation quite well. As always, he was clear beyond a normal conception of clarity, and illuminated things that anthropologists have been wondering about for decades as almost a matter of course, as though he had no idea or interest in the fact that Westerners are unable to easily figure any of this out.

"This means we will be paying a visit to doña Celestina," I inferred with trepidation.

"Exactly," he responded. "That is our business in San Luis today."

"How could you possibly know in advance that I would Dream of her patio?" I shrieked defensively.

"I Dreamed it and bridged the Dream before you arrived," he told me in a mischievous tone.

I was speechless for a long while, while he just sat there and smirked. We headed east towards Yuma and then took the southerly road through Somerton towards San Luis. Finally I asked him, "How does a woman hold Dreaming in her womb?"

"In the same way that she holds a conception. If she is crystal clear, the Dream will come through perfectly, as though passing through transparent water."

"So it takes sexual energy to do Dreaming?" I followed him quite well.

"Absolutely," he confirmed. "The more the better."

"What about men, then? They don't have wombs."

"A man has to build his womb space, by enticing the spirit of a sacred cave or canyon to come with him. The spirit must continually be honored in order for it to desire to remain with him. This is a problem that many white men have, that essentially imbalances them and ultimately makes them powerless. They dishonor the feminine. No shaman worth his salt would ever do such a thing. A cave or canyon spirit will respond to songs, cries, genuine outpourings of longing, and may be honored with cleansings using sweepings and sacred smokes."

"Is that why you often rake the sand outside your home into beautiful patterns?"

"You see the beauty and the honor of it because there is a whole and healthy womb within you." His tone became soft and poetic.

"What about phallic energy, do women have to build it for some magical purpose?"

"Women already have this energy. Doña Celestina will tell you more about it, if she agrees to let you stay with her for a while."

"I am going to stay with doña Celestina?" My hands began to perspire on the steering wheel.

Don Juan smiled openly, showing his even teeth. "Yes, that apartment I found for you is just for your rest breaks. Most likely you'll be with doña Celestina quite often, much more than you may have anticipated." He searched his khaki shirt pocket and then his trouser pocket for a quarter to give to a small Mexican child selling oranges at the border checkpoint.

"We ought to be there shortly. Turn left at the first street after we're across and then right on the first street past El Tecolote herb shop."

A guard smiled and waved us through the Mexican guard station. It felt surreal, almost as though he were saying good-bye to the reality we were leaving and bidding us into a new one. As always, when approaching doña Celestina's territory, I felt a move into an eerie slow motion. I gripped the wheel as we proceeded into an undulating, almost deep-under-waterlike energy, permeating the length of the solitary, sunlit street.

PRACTICE ONE

DREAM BRIDGING

1. Set up the intent to be lucid within your Dream—that is, to realize that you are Dreaming while in the midst of it. Say to yourself over and over as you fall asleep, "I will realize that I am Dreaming during my Dreams." Select a cue, such as your hands or the sound of your own voice, to trigger the realization. Say to yourself, "Each time I hear my own voice, or see my hands, I will realize that I'm Dreaming."

2. Set a gentle alarm to awaken you after three hours of sleep, and then every two hours following. Awakening several times during the night enables you to have more recent recall of all Dreaming activity and to set yourself to the task again.

3. Once you have attained frequent lucidity, start looking for a preselected object not in your possession, such as a smooth stone. When you find that particular object in Dreaming, begin the search for it in the waking world, knowing that you will succeed, even though it may take time. This object has been signaled by power as an aid to you.

4. Once you find your object of Dreaming in the waking world, you have successfully bridged. Ask permission of the energy to take the object home with you, if this is possible. Set it in a prominent place, so that you may see or feel it as you are falling asleep. If your object is a stone, it may be secured over your umbilical region by rolling it in a sash tied around your midriff. If it is not possible to physically take what you have Dreamed, you may photograph it, touch it or simply remember it.

5. Once you can bridge, you may attempt to bridge anything; a place, a person, an idea, a power, something for the betterment of the world, such as peace. The more you bridge, the more sure and sturdy the foundation becomes, until it is so strong that you may actually walk across it, into Dreaming Awake.

MAKING PEACE
WITH THE ANGRY
MOTHER–FATHER

WE WERE USHERED INTO THE TILED ENTRYWAY BY A young Indian woman who spoke to us furtively in a hushed voice. I immediately gathered that she was one of the doña's "girls," young, often destitute Indian women who come to the border towns from small villages deep within Mexico, hoping for work and opportunity. Doña Celestina had in my knowing rescued more than a few of these young girls, whom she often found begging on the streets. Once in her care, she provided them with room and board in the back area of her patio and taught them household skills which they performed for her to earn their keep. Upon mastering a series of chores to perfection, they would move up to more skilled labor until they had mastered marketable skills and could work as seamstresses or in a domestic capacity. Often then they would leave her home, always with great respect.

Not long after coming to live with doña Celestina, the young women would invariably find out that she functioned in San Luis as a witch, a fact which, in addition to her awesome presence, often caused them to become terrified, as this young girl obviously was. And yet they always stayed, a testimony to the sheer strength and capacity of the doña. It was more than a little evident that this girl was terrified of don Juan as well. She seemed now doubly perplexed, almost ready to faint as she led us to chairs on the sunny patio and brought us glasses of water in silence.

I must admit that neither am I immune to the terror inspired by doña Celestina. Although don Juan had a fierce and awesome presence, which still, even after his death, demands respect, doña Celestina's mere gaze can send a chill into the bones. You never get used to her. She looms shadow-like, and the women in her care whisper and keep to the corners and rafters, out of the line of direct fire, almost like bats.

I began to perspire a bit as we waited, and searched the patio for something to gaze upon that would stabilize me into a state of comfortability. My eyes lit on a small glass tabletop upon which was some exquisite, rainbow-colored beadwork. The Yuman speakers, especially the Mohave, the Yuma, or Kw'tsan as they call themselves, and the Cocopa are historically known for some of the world's finest beadwork, much of which is in museums. Doña Celestina is truly an artist of the finest traditional and visionary order when it comes to the delicate quality of her work. I admired the rattlesnake pattern of the beading, and then it dawned on me: This was the same piece I had seen in my Dreaming. Don Juan smiled at me coyly over the top of his glass of water.

The whole scene swam full tilt as if I were engaged in Dreaming at that very moment. Don Juan interrupted my reverie by telling me that this is Dreaming Awake. He explained that when one bridges the Dream and steps into it, one often begins Dreaming again, as if the synchronicity pulls the physical and energy bodies together into lucidly cocreating the now. His explanation was halted by the unmistakable rustle of a skirt. I braced myself for doña Celestina's impending presence.

"Who's that chattering on my patio?"

Good God! She was even more massive than the last time

I had seen her. It is not her height, which is 5'7", but rather her shadow, which seems to follow her like an enslaved mountain. I cringed.

"Well Juan, what do we have here? How old are you now, 150?"

"One hundred this year," he said, standing and graciously bowing. "And you, my dear?"

"Seventy-nine I think, and going backwards. And who is this?" she interrogated in a disarming way, gazing at me and pretending not to know me. "Oh, this is Mer . . . ilyn." She stumbled over my name, which is difficult to say in Spanish, in a deliberate, sleepy voice, a voice that I had heard her use more than once to literally hypnotize her intended addressee. "I'm going to have to change your name dear, to something that rolls more smoothly off the tongue. Merlina, that's a more slippery Spanish sound. Don't you think?" She now looked me squarely in the eyes.

"It's nice. Yes, I rather like it."

Doña Celestina laughed so hauntingly that a crow cawed from the nearby papaya tree. She stepped over to the table where the beadwork was displayed. "She has courage, there is no denying that, is there Juan? Tell me, Merlina, why have you come to see me again?"

I found it impossible to express the whole convoluted scheme. In fact it was hard to find my tongue for any response whatsoever to that question. It was difficult to formulate a thought as doña Celestina waited through the pregnant empty silence, empowering the moment with each pause. She sat down in a bentwood rocker, crossing her legs underneath her long black skirt as she began rocking and humming to herself a strange tune, one that sounded oddly like the one I had been humming to myself that morning.

All I could think of was the punchline to a Mexican joke. The story is that a painter is commissioned to paint the Last

Supper for a governmental affair. He gets drunk on the night before the painting is due and adds a thirteenth apostle. With sobriety, on the morning before the event, the only way he can think of to resolve his horrendous error in time for the banquet is to add a bubble coming out of the mouth of the thirteenth apostle. In the bubble are written the words "No soy apostele, no soy nada. Nada mas vengo a comer, y despues a la chingada," which rhymes in Spanish and means "I'm not an apostle, I'm a nobody. I've just come to eat, and afterwards to hell I go." I said this in Spanish to doña Celestina.

She literally howled with laughter. For a moment I thought both she and don Juan would fall out of their chairs. With that, she got up and spoke quietly to one of her girls in another part of the house and shortly, a delicious meal was being served to us on the patio. There was roasted goat meat, corn tamales, boiled squash and fresh green jalapeño peppers. "Eat up," she invited. "A deal's a deal." And, after finishing his meal, don Juan rose from the table and left me with her.

Fear did not seem to spoil my appetite. I continued eating slowly after don Juan had left the table. I had never tasted roasted goat so I proceeded cautiously, and I must admit it was superb. The aroma of the meat was somewhat metallic, blended with smoky overtones. The flavor was tangy with a marked roasted quality. The consistency was not unlike dark turkey meat.

Doña Celestina remained at the table, also eating in silence. After she had finished, one of the girls, who had been waiting imperceptibly in the wings throughout the entire meal, brought us cups of coffee with a shocked look of fear on her face. This was perhaps the first time she had seen the doña dine socially with guests. Doña Celestina smiled at me and sipped her steaming coffee. I was still uncomfortable, so I examined the tatted Mexican lace tablecloth and the hand-painted folkloric china, both of which were beautifully festive and exotic, as the young woman cleared away our dirty dishes.

I knew that I now had to muster some courage to break the silence or else we would remain suspended in it until don Juan returned, whenever that might be. "I couldn't help but notice your marvelous beadwork, doña Celestina," I began hopefully.

"Well, thank you Merlina. That piece is the rainbow serpent. It is a yoke, which would traditionally be worn by a man, but I was beading that one for you."

"For me?" I was truly astonished.

Doña Celestina gave a sly smirk. She got up from the head of the long, heavy, wooden outdoor dining table and walked out from under the patio portico into the open garden area. Her dark skirt swished with each step. She stopped when she reached the small glass-topped table, where the piece of beadwork glistened in the sunlight, and motioned for me to follow her over there.

I was overtaken by the brilliance of the midday sun reflected off the multicolored glass beads as I approached. Doña Celestina put the yoke around my neck and sang something in Cocopa to the tune I had heard in Dreaming the night before. "Now," she said. "There is peace between us. You needn't fear me. You've never crossed me. Didn't you know that among the Yuma and the Cocopa, women are outrageous Dreamers? I've followed your every move, Merlina—with great interest, I might add."

I was speechless. For the first time, I could really see doña Celestina. She is so very powerful that she seems dangerous, and yet, like a rattlesnake; if you don't make a false move, she won't strike. It was as though the illusion of shadows had been lifted, as though an inner translucent lid, a veil, had been peeled away from my eyes. I felt that in that one poignant moment, I absorbed volumes about ancient feminine power.

I suddenly realized that don Juan could perceive her in this same way and that it was for this reason that he had so much respect for her. I also saw that the young women in her charge had not reached this revelation, and yet they respected her ferocity and power as someone who could teach them to defend themselves against the terrors of a harsh life. I resolved to ask her about these multiple perceptions, but first I thanked her profoundly for the marvelous gift and for the sumptuous feast. We took our coffee with us to the bentwood rockers and seated ourselves comfortably in the shade of the papaya tree.

"Doña Celestina, if you will forgive me, I'll be direct. You scare the wits out of half of the people in this town, out of everyone who has ever had any dealings with you. You make your living as a witch, among other things. And yet now, somehow, I feel that you have been misunderstood."

"I'll be more direct," she replied. "I haven't been misunderstood one bit. I am exactly what you perceived me to be and more. Those people who fear me have good reason to do so. Do people who live near a live volcano not fear? What is your point?"

"No doña Celestina, what is yours?"

"Ah, I see what you mean. You want me to explain myself. Very well, Merlina. I will tell you what you want to know, but slowly. You will have to stay here with me for a while and learn the mysteries. What I have to share is for all women, for men, and of the Earth. Do you agree?"

She weaves just like a spider, I thought to myself, and yet now I feel that I can trust her. "Yes, doña Celestina. I agree. Thank you for inviting me."

She turned her rocker to face me more directly. I marveled at her long, bronzed native face, lined and yet somehow smooth, crowned by the black scarf she often wore as a turban to keep her lustrous silvery hair in place. "You feel that you have seen a different side of me now, is that it?"

"Yes, it is."

"Think of what Earth was like before people started to misunderstand her power and treat her with disrespect. She was pure, powerful, sometimes volatile and harsh during times of change, but wise, life-giving, abundant. There was never any doubt who had the final say. The Earth was in charge. She could be ferocious when needed, but she shared that ferocity with her chosen. The Earth is a survivor, she will fight, but she also knows peace." She began to rock in the chair slowly.

"Now there is doubt about who has control. There is abuse of power, corruption, pollution. But I assure you the control is still in the same place and the Earth is growing fangs, in case she needs to use them. What I do is merely a reflection of the powers I wield, female powers that come straight from the Earth. Those who fear and dread me merely see a reflection of the repercussions of their unclean ways. Those who are at peace with me realize that a strong female is always responsible for the best males and females, and for the best balance of life on Earth. A strong female, if she is balanced by the virtue of her power, has strong love and loves strength. She creates strength in love and there is balance and peace. If there is imbalance, there is anger and reason to fear.

"The difference between a witch and an ordinary powerful woman is that the witch knows the mysteries she wields and from whence they come. The ordinary woman is like a powerful car, powerful because she has a dynamic engine, and yet she does not know how she works and looks to the man to tinker on her, make her repairs and know how to operate her controls. Can you imagine that the Earth would ever forget how she works? Or could she forget that she is the one who gives life and teaches about its maintenance?

"Well, neither would the witch, but this is the plight of ordinary women. And this is why both ordinary men and ordinary women fear what they call witches, a name meant to evoke terror. Powerful men of knowledge do not fear, but rather respect powerful female wise women. Look at the way that Juan behaves. There is not an ounce of fear in him, and yet there is caution and respect, as well there should be. He is one of the best males I have ever seen. That is the way males can turn out when women are allowed to be what they should be."

Hearing doña Celestina speak, as an older Indian woman, about don Juan, as a representative of the male species, was rather uncharted terrain for me as a woman much younger than either of them. "I know that he lost his mother when he was eleven or twelve and also his father, and that when he was very young he had one grandmother who had lived a traditional life before the whites arrived in this area for the gold rush," I interjected.

"In those days, boys were men at twelve. They had their initiation ceremonies into manhood and ran for four days and nights seeking vision. Life was more balanced and the world of power was part of everyday life for all. We were at peace with this harsh desert and lived here comfortably. The men and women grew tall, the men, often well over six feet. We all had straight bones, decay-free teeth, and long healthy lives. There were many who lived to 110 or 115 years without suffering senility or weakness. There are still a few. All the men wore long mud-rolled hair to honor the Earth. We were a fierce people and still are, and yet we could know peace. That is what we come from. I would say that if Juan's mother had to leave the Earth while he was still young, she picked the right time to do it.

"The whites who first saw this desert were terrified of it, and rightly so. It can appear hostile, and if you do not live a clean and balanced life here it will dry you up. And yet only in the solitude and open spaces of this beautiful, colorful desert can one truly expand and sense all that there is, the emptiness, the life, death, survival, wisdom and power."

"Your name Soledad, solitude, suits you perfectly," I exclaimed, moved by the metaphors of the magnificent desert. I truly felt at peace with her. She was like the primordial female creator–destroyer, complete, mother–father, male and female in one, somehow dragonlike.

It had grown to be late afternoon while we talked. Doña Celestina got up from her rocker and motioned for me to follow her down the long corridor on the right side of her patio. Stopping outside one of the doors, she showed me to a bedroom which was to be my own during my stay with her. The cool, shaded room seemed so enticing that I decided to take a siesta.

PRACTICE TWO

MAKING PEACE WITH THE ANGRY
MOTHER–FATHER

1. Make an offering of apology to the female–male creative
   principle, and to the Earth. This offering may be in the
   form of a prayer bundle, a ceremony, or an especially written song. Select your offering by intending to Dream it,
   and then by bridging what has been shown to you. If you
   receive a song, then sing it. If you find the items of your
   prayer bundle in Dreaming, then look for them in the waking world in order to create it. Perhaps you will hear the
   prayer you are to offer, or will see the ceremony you are
   to perform.
2. Take your offering to a sacred place that speaks to you of
   creation and that you feel invites you to offer this energy.
   There you may leave your carefully crafted prayer bundle,
   which should contain small items that represent your
   covenant of peace and renewal. You may offer your prayer.
   Your ceremony may be conducted here, perhaps to include
   offerings to the elements and powers of nature. If your gift
   is a song, sing or play it with feeling while burning copal or
   sacred tobacco.
3. Finally, leave your intent in the place. Perhaps voice it
   aloud, and then voice your thanks. Walk away quietly, with
   a silent mind full of gratitude.

RECAPITULATION

I AWOKE ASTONISHED THAT I HAD SLEPT THE ENTIRE evening and throughout the night without stirring even once. The sun was just beginning to come up rather than to go down. Morning birds were making tentative calls, seemingly asking if light was emerging. Stepping out into the passageway and crossing the patio into the kitchen, I softly told one of the young girls who was already up, dressed, and making tortillas by hand, that I was going out to my jeep to get a few things.

I quietly moved the jeep off the street and in back of doña Celestina's home. Bringing in some of my belongings, I tiptoed to the garden shower in the back area of the patio and had hot water for the first time in forty-eight hours. Showering outdoors among the desert flora, the birds, and the large tropical papaya which had to be watered and steamed often, was close to paradise. When I was dressed, I went into the kitchen.

The young woman was working silently and had probably been up since 4:00 in the morning, judging by the amount of tortillas she had made and the pristine cleanliness of the kitchen. It was obvious that she was fearful of being caught talking without working and tried to answer me only briefly and in whispers while she worked, never looking me fully in the eye.

I asked what I should call her. She told me that her name was Amalita and that she was Mixtec from Oaxaca, but that the doña called her Mala, a funny nickname for Amalita, because it is a play on words that means "bad girl." She could not have been more than fifteen. With coaxing, she said that she had come to San Luis looking for work and that she had been selling chicle, chewing gum, on the street corner when doña Celestina had passed by and asked her about herself. Mala described herself to me as an orphan who was uneducated, unmarried, and did not yet have any babies, but there was a man in her village who had been at her. She ran from the village to get away from him, only to find more hardship, as one can well imagine.

Mala then told me that the "señor," don Juan, had returned the prior evening and that he was sleeping in the bedroom at the head of the passageway. She seemed reluctant to say anything else about any of us, especially doña Celestina, and did not appear to want me to tell her anything about don Juan or myself. I was informed that there were three other girls in the house besides herself, and that she had been in the doña's home for five months. Two of the girls had been there for several years, and the newest girl for just a month and a half. Chencha was her name and she was already washing sheets at the scrub basin, in the wash area behind the patio. The other girls were Neida and Pacha, and they were sweeping and mopping, but they were also learning to sew and often did the shopping.

As if to change the subject, Mala politely informed me that the doña had ordered Chinese black tea with ginseng root before breakfast and asked me if I cared for a cup. I accepted, although I was shocked that doña Celestina had a taste or the purse for Chinese tea, especially when I saw that the ginseng was a fine-quality, large, aged root. Mala quietly explained to me that there was a small Chinese community in San Luis, who had excellent restaurants, of which I was already aware. The owner of the finest, she whispered, had come to doña Celestina for a "trabajito"—literally a little job—in this case an act of witchcraft. She then showed me tins of first-quality Gunpowder and Lapsang Souchang teas and two lucky cat statues, a black and a white. Doña Celestina had also received money and an intricately carved wooden staff, Mala recounted with sheer amazement.

Mala's face then fell in horror as she realized that she had let the cat out of the bag and spoken too much, especially about something that was not permitted. I told her not to worry, that I knew that doña Celestina's longevity and her talents had brought her a wide array of acquaintances and experiences. And, I added with emphasis, the same was true for the "señor." Mala's jaw dropped. She had suspected as much. She was in double trouble now. Hastily, as if to cover up, she told me that the normal morning's beverage was a tea made of ephedra, which grows wild in the dry water canyons of the area. I went back to my room with my teacup, snickering softly to myself.

After breakfasting alone some time later, I was in my bedroom writing in my journal. I thought that I heard don Juan moving things around in the patio area, so I quickly put the notebook into a drawer of the old medical desk in my room and went out to see what was going on. I was filled with questions about Dreaming male and female energy, overflowing after the past two days' experiences. On the way, I picked up from the nightstand the beaded yoke that doña Celestina had given me, for don Juan to examine more closely.

"Don Juan, did you see this?" I blurted in amazement as he stooped to move the glass-topped table and rockers to a shady place under the portico, and cleared a large area under the papaya tree. I handed him the beadwork and he nodded with admiration, handling the delicate piece gently and turning it to and fro in the morning sunlight.

"Do you know the significance of the design?" he asked me in return.

"All doña Celestina has told me so far is that the pattern is that of the rainbow serpent," I replied, curious for more detail.

"A long time ago," don Juan responded, "seers perceived that the serpent is the guardian of the realms of evolution. For female shamans, to have the serpent as their spirit helper is a most desirable thing. Among the Yuma, girls sought the serpent in their puberty initiations."

"A marked contrast to Adam and Eve," I joked.

Don Juan laughed. "Fear of our own nature can be our worst enemy."

"The snake was so often linked to wisdom, sexual energy, longevity and transformation in shamanic and esoteric traditions. Why was the early Judeo-Christian story of creation so twisted?" I couldn't account for the discrepancy and voiced my thoughts aloud.

"Perhaps it has something to do with the serpent itself," don Juan proposed. "In our tradition, the snake is the guardian of the feminine, the guardian of caves, rock crevices, and of the womb. Snake power is female."

"Aha! I see. They were dumping the Goddess!" I shouted.

Doña Celestina walked through the patio at that precise moment. She smiled broadly at me, almost leering as she passed. Skirt swishing, she made her way to the sewing room where Neida and Pacha awaited her. I was awestruck.

"What do you think the rainbow represents?" don Juan asked me, twirling the shimmering multicolored necklace before my eyes like a hypnotist.

In my mind's eye I saw the spiraling double helix. I gasped. "Ancient shamans saw DNA?" I cried out.

"Dreaming is the world's most powerful microscope, or telescope, or screen. A trained Seer can witness anything, but only with sobriety and discernment can one extract wisdom from the view. Otherwise, it's all smoking mirrors. The first act of Seeing clearly with discernment is to clean the windows, if you will, of all preconceptions. That is the magical act we will perform today, right here in this open space.

"We are going to have a *Ku'ruk*, a ceremony of recapitulation, in which we recall all of the ways that the feminine has been burdened and dethroned. We will place our acts of recapitulation that recount all of these trials on a pyre that I will build here, and we will watch them burn while we sing of her glories and her triumphs."

There was a sound of power in his voice that gave me chills, as though he were invoking the primordial sexuality that existed before the very first spark. "You like to write, so that is how you will do your recapitulation. Today you will See and write the creation, the story of how this whole thing began and how it changed. You will write the story to be burned, and in so doing the powers will return to their proper places. Doña Celestina and I will do the same task according to our tradition, and at twilight we will meet here again to recount and to burn it all."

A sudden wind kicked up, signaling that it would be a dusty day. I retreated to my bedroom to write, so that I would not be disturbed by the wind or dust. The task was a daunting one which I took quite seriously. Rather than a list that I myself was creating, the assignment seemed to choose its own course. It was rather as though the long-silent feminine power within myself had finally agreed to speak. What I had thought would be a harangue, came out rather like a first-hand narrative account of creation, stating plainly each place where the sacred feminine had been dispossessed and, as a result, had left us. I was in tears in places and felt that I might not be able to go on with it, but the cleansing, clearing intent of the task always reasserted its imperative and lent me sobriety.

I spent the entire day working and, when twilight was imminent, I had filled an entire notebook, with the exception of the last few pages. At twilight the words, feelings, and images simply stopped, as though the appointed hour was recognized by the energy itself. I walked over to the old wash-stand placed against one wall of my room and filled the ceramic bowl with cool water from the pitcher on its marble top. Splashing my face prepared and revived me. I gathered my notebook and walked out into the evening.

Under the papaya tree, a large pile of sand had been placed, and on top of that, a small pyre had been built. Don Juan and doña Celestina were already standing nearby, for they had, in fact, just ignited the kindling. Each of them held in their hands a small figure that they had made. Don Juan allowed me to hold his. It was appalling to the touch, a carved wooden figure of about three inches in height, shriveled, deformed, bent over and wrinkled. He called it *K'tar*, blind old man. Doña Celestina then handed me her figurine, which was a clay doll, a female covered with red paint, naked with a snake emerging from her abdomen.

I handed them my notebook in turn. They each felt the weight of it and flipped through the pages to see the rippling cursive flow front and back. Nodding in approval, it seemed that both were aware of the contents without having asked me to read from it aloud. Don Juan then began to sing a series of mythic song cycles in native tongues. Doña Celestina followed him, tapping her feet. The fire began to blaze and a moment came for her to place the female figurine into the fire in a standing position.

Don Juan's song then seemed to change into a lament and he placed the wooden carving to face the clay doll. Now they sang back and forth as though there were a battle between the two figurines that were outlined in fire as the tempo and the tension rose. First the snake broke off the belly of the female doll. Then the male burned. Finally the female exploded in a loud, shattering pop. The song that don Juan and doña Celestina sang was then truly sad and tears were in their eyes.

After that cycle, they asked me to put my notebook into the fire unread. It made perfect sense to me and I did so willingly and with reverence. The tone of the songs again changed, this time to one of hope and release. There was singing until the last smoldering cinder had given up the ghost, when we heard the call of an owl and the breeze turned cold. Doña Celestina signaled that we should leave the patio and go to our rooms for a while. Then she hurriedly motioned for two of her girls to come and clean up the ashes.

Several hours later there was a knock at my door. I came out to find that all of the furniture had been replaced on the patio. Another fire had been built under the papaya tree and this time a cauldron was steaming, just as I had seen it my Dream, only this scene was at night and all was dark. I walked over to the cauldron to peek at what was inside. Fresh corn kernels and rice were gently simmering in water laced with night-blooming jasmine blossoms.

We were served and we all sat in rockers, eating the creamy, flavorful porridge under the stars. The temperature had mysteriously become less chilly. Night birds were singing with abandon and a waxing moon was up. "We won't speak of this again," doña Celestina began from her seat, "so if you have any questions, you had better ask them."

I looked over at her in the moonlight. She was rocking as peacefully as a soft breeze. I thought of the relationship between women and the wind, knowing that doña Celestina normally blows northerly. I felt the change of direction.

"Have we appeased some force by our ceremony tonight?" I asked. "How else can I account for the changes in mood that we experienced? It was as if we had ingested sacred plants in a *mitote* [an all-night ceremony, a vision quest in which ritual

participants ingest the peyote cactus, a powerful hallucino-
gen, and seek Dreaming, visions, and guidance, accompanied
by ritual purification, songs and fire ceremony]. All of us
were affected by waves of energy in the same way at certain
moments."

"Dreaming together can be very like a *mitote*. Individual
awareness merges with a heightened awareness that is shared.
What we shared is real," don Juan replied.

"The cleansing, however, was the most important part for
you," doña Celestina added. "Now we can approach everything afresh. As Juan has been telling you, our sexual energies
are very important to magical work. A thorough recapitulation is necessary, and more than that, a purification. We had
to burn away the dead illusion and prepare you."

"Prepare me for what?"

"Well, for one thing, Chon will be here tomorrow." Doña
Celestina smiled.

"Chon, here?" I reeled.

"Yes, and you know how the Maya expect one to be clean
before they begin anything serious." She laughed out loud.

"What . . . why . . . how is it possible that Chon is coming
to San Luis?"

"He comes about once every three years to trade medicinal
plants and recipes with the hierbero [herbalist] of El Tecolote.
That shop is known by healers, herbalists and witches throughout Mexico. Didn't you know that's how we met?" don Juan
answered casually. "Once, a long time ago, when we were both
young, I had brought in some Datura, and Chon arrived while
I was there, looking for some to use in a ceremony. We struck
up a conversation and a long acquaintance, and, as you know,
we've been friends ever since."

"But Chon knows doña Celestina?" I tried to ask respectfully.

"Of course," she said. "*Curanderos* [healers] and *brujas* [witches, sorceresses] often have dealings with one another. He's going to stay in the house while he conducts his business at El Tecolote."

"This is incredible! All four of us are going to be under one roof?" Up until that moment, there had never been an instance when all of us were able to be together at one time and place. I was elated and extremely excited by the possibilities. Chon was coming from the jungle highlands of Chiapas to the desert of Sonora! It was more than I could have hoped. And he was going to be here tomorrow.

PRACTICE THREE

RECAPITULATION

1. Write down the entire event or situation from which you wish to withdraw your energy, reexamining it moment by moment, including every detail. Concentrate on one event, person, or situation at a time, focusing on the most problematic and critical areas of your life first.

2. When you have completed the writing, create a ceremonial fire and burn the entire work. Breathe the warmth of the fire in through your nostrils and down into an expanded abdomen. This warmth and glow is your energy, being freed and released by the flames in order to come back to you cleansed.

3. When the fire is just smoldering ashes, breathe in the last of the glow and exhale forcefully through the nostrils, pushing the abdomen in on the exhale and sweeping the head to the right. This exhale releases all attachments to the experience and scatters the ashes of it to be further cleansed and recycled by the Earth.

4. Once the fire is completely out, collect the remaining cooled ashes and either bury them or scatter them over a body of water, saying a prayer of forgiveness and release.

4

EXPLORING
CELIBACY

THE NEXT MORNING, I COULD SCARCELY CONTAIN MY enthusiasm. Neida and Pacha had gone shopping to prepare for the impending arrival of another guest. Doña Celestina was in consultation in her altar room and don Juan had gone to see a friend in town. In search of something to do to keep my mind off of my excitement, I helped Chencha with her ironing. We were listening to Mexican ranchera music and to *corridos* as we dripped water from bowls with our fingertips onto the collars of blouses and steam-pressed them beautifully crisp. This corrido was about Cesar Chavez, an agricultural hero who had been born near Yuma, Arizona. I knew some of the words, so I sang what I knew in an exaggerated way and hummed the rest.

"Cerca de Yuma Ari-zooooona . . ."

Chencha giggled, revealing a broken front tooth. I smiled back at her in wonder. She was perhaps even younger than Mala, thirteen or fourteen I'd say, though I didn't ask. She was Papago, from the area around Yepachic in the mountains of Sonora. Her situation was similar to Mala's, though it was hunger that had driven her from her village to take her first job working in the lettuce fields. She had met doña Celestina in San Luis early one morning not so long ago while standing in near darkness, waiting for the worker bus at one of the field hand pickup points.

Doña Celestina had just been to the local bakery, which opens in the wee hours of the morning with the first batch of fresh baked rolls. Chencha smelled bread in the doña's basket, and though she didn't intend for doña Celestina to notice her desire, she did. Doña Celestina stopped on the corner and offered Chencha a hot roll, which she rapidly ate voraciously and gratefully. Admiring the girl's hunger, the doña told her that she had some work in her home and that there would be many such rolls, that she would even teach Chencha to bake them herself. There was a room if Chencha wanted to follow her now, which she did without looking back.

Pondering the story as I ironed, I couldn't help but admire the doña's style. The old witch with food in her basket routine, that was priceless. I could see the whole scene as though I were floating above it. Doña Celestina, the perfect crone; Chencha the perfect hungry, innocent young girl devouring the hot roll, while the old witch rubs her hands in sinister anticipation. "Want to follow me, young girly?"

The difference, of course, whether or not doña Celestina wants to admit it, is that she actually cares about these disenfranchised young women. And more than that, which she will readily admit, she teaches them something useful. Surviving as an older Indian woman, who has successfully lived on her own for decades, could not have been anything other than a horrendous effort. Doña Celestina has volumes to teach to anyone who is willing to learn, yet she always selects girls who are most in need, but who, at the same time, have the courage not to feel sorry for themselves.

Despite my pleasure in Chencha's company and in my ruminations, the ironing didn't help the morning pass any faster. I kept thinking of Chon, about what time he might arrive, how he would appear in this southwestern desert, what stories he would have to tell and if there was an ulterior motive for his visit, which despite don Juan's casual comments seemed quite portentous to me. Chencha sensed my agitation and, since we had almost finished with the ironing, she told me that the doña had instructed her to invite me into the altar room if I seemed restless.

I was astounded. I had never been present during one of doña Celestina's consultations before. We had always talked about the work after the fact. Putting my ironing board and iron away first, I went to my room to freshen up and then sat in one of the chairs outside doña Celestina's consultation room, as a client was also doing. Not wanting to interrupt something in progress, I waited until the heavy wooden door opened and a short Mexican man exited.

The female client who was seated outside the door looked at me questioningly. I rose from my chair and motioned for her to enter the dark workroom alongside of me. We entered and I could smell the faint hint of a smoke that I was not quite able to place. It had an immediate tranquilizing effect. Doña Celestina sat backed by her altar table on which a tall, thick red candle stood burning. She acknowledged both our presences with a nod of her head and motioned for me to sit to her left in a chair positioned unobtrusively along the wall. The client sat directly before doña Celestina.

This slight Mestizo woman, who appeared to be perhaps thirty-five years of age, was very nervous and fidgeted under doña Celestina's cold scrutiny. She held a rosary in her hands, which were folded discreetly on her lap. She quietly worked through the rosary and twisted it tightly around her fingers.

"Yes?" doña Celestina waited.

The woman swallowed a huge lump of fear and stammered to speak. "First, with all due respect . . ." She paused. "I want to say that I never would have come to see you, Ma'am, if I weren't completely desperate." Her voice shook. "I was raised a Catholic, you see, and I've prayed to God over and over . . . but to no avail." Tears welled in her eyes and her delicate features were stricken. "A friend of my mother's told me about you, Ma'am. It was she who suggested that I bring my problem to you." She stopped for a long moment as her jaw began trembling.

Doña Celestina sat back in her chair and folded crossed arms below her chest. She sighed softly, glowering at the shivering woman, whose appearance was reduced to that of a naked child sitting in a cold wind. The doña turned slowly and took the red candle off of her altar to place it on the floor between them. This seemed to warm the woman and give her the fluidity and confidence to speak more of her troubles. The light of the candle cast long shadows across both of them, exaggerating the blackness of doña Celestina's attire and the pallor of fear worn by the woman. She struggled to begin again.

"I was a widow with three children when I married my second husband," she confided. "We were destitute and I felt that we needed protection from someone who would help provide for us. I was in love with my first husband, but I must admit that in the case of my second, I married without love. I was more attractive in those days and he had work and was willing to accept the children. I let those details guide my choice. Now I see that I was so very wrong. It is from my husband that we most need protection.

"At first it was just a matter of occasional beatings when he would come home drunk, and there were other women. I thought we could stand these things because he brought in the money for our household. I felt guilty that perhaps I was deserving of this treatment because I lacked passion for him. After each incident, I always went to the priest to confess and to ask advice, and I prayed that the love would come to me and that my husband's ways would mend.

"When my husband began to notice my thirteen-year-old daughter, I told myself that it was my fault. I tried to make everything just the way he likes in the home and there was peace for a while. Then suddenly my daughter became sullen and withdrawn and refused to talk with me about it. The change showed in her personal appearance. She seemed ashamed and frightened and she wouldn't discuss it.

"Now matters have become worse. I am almost certain that he is molesting her. She says nothing, but my husband is more belligerent at home than ever. I feel that he has stolen her soul. She is whipped, empty, as though she were possessed. I went to the priest and accused my husband in confession, hoping that the Church would intercede on my daughter's behalf. I think that the priest did not even believe me. Perhaps after all, he is just a man. He offered prayers to help me make the right decisions.

"I can't go to the police because I have no proof and my daughter will not speak out. Besides, the police are all men. If I accuse my husband myself, he will beat us within an inch of our lives, and if I try to leave . . . well, we have nowhere else to go. He owns everything now. My mother is dead, so I can't return to her home. I'm sure that if I try to take my daughter away from him, something terrible will happen. I know he has threatened her."

"What do you want me to do?" doña Celestina requested somberly.

"I'm afraid to ask for your help. I fear I have lost my soul by marrying this man. I don't know where my desperation can possibly lead."

"What kind of help are you looking for?" doña Celestina pressed, with focused intent.

"I need for him to leave us, to go away from this place and leave us in peace in our home! I can get a job in one of the sewing factories. I know that I can. My mother's *comadre* [best friend] does this work and she has been teaching me. I was told that you can make him leave us, that you are able to enter dreams and . . . but . . ."

"You are afraid that I need the Devil to do it," doña Celestina completed her thought. "Let me relieve you of that burden, my dear. I don't."

"Oh, doña Celestina! You are able to help me then?"

"Yes. Bring me a personal article that belongs to your husband. I'm not going to tell you how I do my work, but during the night while he is dreaming I will bring him here and show him a few things, a few visitors into his dreams while he is asleep and while he's awake. When you return with the item, I'll also give you something to put into his food. It will calm him down and he'll lose interest in sex, become more . . . pliable. Eventually, he will lose interest in everything altogether and he'll leave you. As for your daughter, an acquaintance of mine who is a healer arrives this afternoon. You should bring your daughter to see him tomorrow. I guarantee you the situation will resolve itself."

The woman stood up so rapidly that the rosary fell to the floor. Overwhelmed with desperate hope she cried, "Oh thank you, doña, thank you." I rose to show her the way out and put my arm around her shoulders. She looked up at me through teary eyes that were beaming with gratitude. "She's the real thing, isn't she?" the woman affirmed. I nodded.

After escorting her to the front gate, I reflected on how the recapitulation had completely cleansed my perception and energy, and had enabled me to participate in the consultation with clarity, sobriety and a calm that never would have been possible before, and perhaps most importantly, without judging. Chon always stressed that energetic cleanliness is an essential in receiving the appropriate empowerment and in the maintenance of the energy flow. I looked forward to discussing all of this with him when he arrived.

I didn't have to wait very long, for almost as soon as the woman had walked out the gate, I heard the front bell ring. I ran to the door to let him in myself. "Chon!" I cried, opening my arms for an embrace. He stood there grinning in a canary yellow shirt, jeans, and sandals. Dropping his bag, he went for the hug and roughed up my short hair with his hand, gazing cheerfully into my eyes.

"C'mon in!" I exclaimed. "Doña Celestina is in a consultation now and don Juan is out walking, so I have you all to myself for a while! Let me get you something."

Chon sat down in one of the rockers while I brought him a cool glass of fresh limeade made with honey. "How was your journey?" I asked, handing him the large tumbler.

"Long, dusty and beautiful," he replied with a smile. "Ah!" He relaxed back and took a look around at the patio. Then his eyes came to rest on me and he examined me curiously, as if I were a rare species of desert flora. "What have you been up to in Dreaming, my little doe?" My awareness shifted to fully bridging the Dream of doña Celestina's patio, now that he was here.

I giggled and told him everything, especially what had taken place since my arrival at don Juan's house. It was obviously a delight for Chon to exact so much detail. He kept gently probing with his eyes and with his smiles, seemingly quite invigorated by the excitement of this visit. After satisfying his almost endless curiosity, he pronounced that I held a Dream perfectly. I then recounted the recapitulation and narrated the morning's consultation, remembering the questions I had for him about it.

"Well, Merlina," he said playfully, as if happy to oblige, using the new name doña Celestina had given me, "I see that you are all grown up and discovering the connection between sexual energy, Dreaming, and healing." He was putting me on and teasing me about my question. "You really put an old man on the spot. Especially after such a long journey!" He rocked in his chair, feigning exhaustion. As usual, Chon's humor was joyful and completely dismissed any seriousness found lurking in me. I fluidly adjusted rather than becoming off balance. It occurred to me that we were outrageous Dreamers, that this was a Dream we were Dreaming awake, but somehow my intent shifted me and I was more interested in what he had to say. He sensed this and shifted as well. I then remembered that perhaps his greatest capacity as a healer is to transmit joy within the energy and yet efficiently do his work.

"Your question is about energetic cleanliness, am I correct?" His tone became sober. "I can tell you what the Maya see, since I was born into that culture. We see that to serve as a Day Keeper for one's days in the calendar count, or as a Lineage Head for a village, or to be a H'men, the highest order of healer-priest, requires energetic cleanliness and potency, including abstention from sexual relations on those occasions when one serves in an extraordinary capacity within the community. This is in order to see and to bring the energy through in a pure form.

"Shamanic Dreaming practices undertaken by the Maya, such as shifting, or energetic healing work, require a lot of cleansed sexual energy, and they evolve it, arousing and transforming it upward. This is not to say that human relations are unclean in their best possible expressions, but they are entangled. A practitioner seeks to free up large quantities of cleansed energy for its evolution. His or her desire blossoms and expands to meet the energies that are presenting themselves—powers, spirits, openings into other worlds.

"Practitioners who care for one another share these energies in ways that also refine and evolve. This may be together and it may become a love relationship with great mysteries, beingness, and creation itself. What happens is that the sexual response to energy definitely changes, and it is supposed to do so. The refined energies concentrate and begin to grow upward toward life and awareness, rather than toward death.

"That's an important point. Sexual energy is one of the primordial energies of creation and evolution. Unfortunately, though, for the ordinary person, by the time they find this out—if they ever do—their energy has already been used in producing the status quo. They're all used up."

We both had to laugh. "This is why I recommend to my male and female apprentices, as you know," he nudged, "that they contain their sexual urges until something better comes along. We should be searching for expressions of sexuality that are evolved, long lived and ecstatic, not harmful.

"My personal preference is for Dreaming. As Juancho has no doubt been telling you, it takes a great deal of sexual energy to Dream because Dreaming accesses art and energy of creation. My other predilection, one not chosen by me but with which I am in complete agreement, is for healing. These are the gardens where my flowers bloom, where my intimacies occur; private paradise that I encounter and sometimes share with others like yourself."

PRACTICE FOUR

CLEANSING THE SEXUAL ENERGY

1. Explore the nature of energetic attachments that are created through sexual intercourse. These may be Seen as fibers, like tentacles that attach your creative energy into the manifestational potential of your partner or partners. Ask yourself if you wish for your creative energies to be applied in this way.

2. If you desire to extricate yourself from an energetic entanglement of this nature, you must first, of course, curtail all sexual relations with the partner or partners from whom you wish to remove your energy.

3. A thorough recapitulation of each individual then follows. (See Recapitulation, page 32.)

4. Following the recapitulation, you must analyze the pattern that was created by the energetic fibers of attachment and why it was undesirable. Then you must strive not to repeat it. The recapitulation will give you a sufficient boost of energy to aid you in your task and in the disassembly of the pattern.

5. A period of sober celibacy following this, or loyalty to a very intimate and trustworthy partner, coupled with additional recapitulation, will further cleanse, disentangle and renew the energies.

RETRIEVING OUR LOST ENERGY

AFTER DON JUAN RETURNED FROM HIS WALK around San Luis and doña Celestina had finished her consultations, which she only took during the days beginning each week, we all put ourselves to the task of preparing a feast in honor of Chon's arrival from the Yucatan. Pacha and Neida had bought several chickens which we prepared Yucatecan style, by surrounding them in yams, mangos, papaya, onions, tomatoes, and spices, wrapping the mixture in fresh banana leaves and setting it all to steam in a clay pot until the meat is so tender that it falls off the bones.

The atmosphere became very festive, almost exotic, with Chon's distinct presence added to the group. Neida, Pacha, and I began dancing as we mashed black beans to make refritos. There was laughter and story-telling from the patio. At twilight the meal was almost ready. We set up the heavy wooden table under the patio portico for the guests, and another smaller wooden table in the kitchen for the four girls.

The food was so delicious that everyone concentrated on savoring it at first, but later, as appetites dimmed, Chon began to grace the table with more of his delightful tales. Some were funny, others were serious, dealing with impending Mayan revolution in the state of Chiapas. The best by far had to do with a famous transsexual show queen by the name of Eufemia, who happened to once have been a patient of Chon's.

The story goes that Eufemia was born Eufemio, to a Mayan family in a Yucatecan village often visited by Chon, after Chon had left Guatemala due to the massacres of Maya there. A poor little boy of almost other-worldly beauty, Eufemio preferred to learn household chores with his mother and sisters rather than to go out and run with the other boys of the village. This was not a problem for his family or for the other families in the small town.

However, when Eufemio was six his father took a job making *hamacas*—hammocks—in the large city of Merida, capital of the state of Yucatan. His father moved the family there and Eufemio had the opportunity to go to school. On the first day the teacher asked the boys and girls to line up separately and Eufemio lined up with the girls, insisting that he was one. The children all laughed and the teacher tried to force him gently into the other line. He resisted tenaciously, telling her that it was she who was making the mistake.

The teacher complained to Eufemio's mother when she arrived, walking from their little home to the Primaria that afternoon to pick him up. The family was distressed to realize that it was not merely a matter of preference; their child didn't recognize the difference between himself and little girls and did not seem to grasp the concept of male and female.

At the first opportunity, Eufemio's mother sought out a shaman healer-priest for the child to talk with. She found Chon at the Indian market behind a stand, selling his herbal remedies. At first seeing, Chon realized that the boy was exceptional. Upon scanning his body energetically, talking with him and, later, watching him grow and develop, Chon came to the conclusion that the young person was more female than male.

The idea of judging wasn't in Chon's vocabulary. He simply advised Eufemio on numerous matters and often did *limpias*—energetic cleansings—to remove the negative effects of the teasing that the boy constantly received. They spoke about aspects of female warriorship and Chon taught Eufemio not to indulge in drama.

By the time he had turned fifteen, Eufemio was a stunning beauty, outshining many of the girls he associated with. One night while walking home from the cinema, he was attacked by a group of adolescent boys and after that resolved to run away to a place where no one would know his personal history. He decided to flee to Mexico City, lose himself in the multitude and live life as a woman, without anyone there knowing that he possessed a penis.

Life was not so easy at first, but Eufemia's beauty was undeniable. The Mexican men suggested that she become a show girl in one of the flashy clubs of the Zona Rosa, not realizing that, unclothed, she possessed no breasts. Finally Eufemia realized that she would have to face her ambiguous sexuality, and she did what she was able. She became a show girl in a drag review. From time to time, when Chon came through Mexico City on his way to the nearby town of Toluca to trade herbs at the Tuesday Indian market there, he would look Eufemia up, to make sure she was all right, and would bring news of her home to her family when he passed through their village.

Her fame as a drag show queen slowly began to rise. Even though straight Mexican men sometimes saw the show for a laugh, or so they said, both they and the gay men who frequented the club had to admit that Eufemia was prettier than any of the "real" women on stage at the other night clubs. When Chon would pass through town, he would say prayers to the nine Mayan lords of the night for her success.

Success became Eufemia, and eventually the review was

invited to Rio de Janeiro, Brazil, for a guest appearance. The audience and the club owner fell in love with Eufemia and so she was able to remain in this more cosmopolitan environment, where she increased her earnings twenty-fold. Eventually she was able to finance a complete sex change operation. The best at that time were done in Brazil, and when she finally returned to Mexico, it was as a svelte yet exquisitely curvaceous and dignified female.

When Chon saw her again, she was the star of an all-female gala in one of Mexico City's top straight night clubs. She thanked him profusely for all he had done for her and told him that if she could ever return the favor, she gladly would. Several years later, she had the opportunity. At that time, a political official of the state of Jalisco who had heard of Chon through a young friend, a Mexican anthropologist who had worked among the Maya and now lived in Mexico City, requested an appointment with Chon while they were both in the capital.

To Chon's dismay, this self-inflated politico boasted of how he had seen his young wife through breast cancer and a double mastectomy thanks to his "financial in" with the Mexican government. Now he was going to buy her new breasts, so that she could feel and appear as beautiful as she once had been. He was actually there for a *Primicia*, a Mayan ceremony of blessing upon a new venture and upon the health of his wife, in that order.

Chon told him that he would be happy to work for the continued well-being of the young woman, but wanted to know why new breasts were required. Hadn't she been through enough? The government official told Chon in no uncertain terms that the new breasts were necessary in order for him to demonstrate his continued affection for his wife in the most intimate manner possible. At that point, Chon laughed in his face.

"It doesn't bother you that they'll be artificial?" he asked.

The man replied that it did not, but that the reconstructive surgery was complicated and it was for this reason that he had requested the blessing.

At this point doña Celestina interjected, "I'm surprised he didn't ask for a blessing on his pecker, to help him raise it up. I get that request all the time."

We were all falling out of our chairs and pounding on the table as Chon tried to continue. I couldn't help but think of the look on the face of the Mexican man who'd been leaving doña Celestina's consultation room before I entered that morning, wondering if that was what he had been up to. And that if it was, no doubt doña Celestina had shrunk him like a spider on a hot stove.

Chon covered his large smile with his hands, took a deep breath, shook his head, covered his eyes and then his ears and finally, after recovering himself, began to recount more of the tale. "Very well," he told the man, "but before I do the blessing, there is an acquaintance of mine that I wish for you to go see. Her name is Eufemia. She is a famous night club performer, very beautiful. She once had the operation you are speaking about, and is as attractive as the most desirable woman on Earth. She will do me a favor and show you her breasts. They are a work of the gods. If you are able to get excited then I will be satisfied and do the blessing for you."

The politico was practically salivating as Chon wrote down the posh address for him and gave him instructions. "Don't visit until tomorrow at about 2:00 P.M. She performs at night and likes her sleep in the mornings. I'll phone Eufemia personally and ask her to be expecting you." I braced myself for the story of this encounter, which I knew would send us all to the floor.

The next afternoon, the married politician arrived at the luxurious high-rise apartment building where Eufemia resided, bedecked in his best suit with brilliantine in his hair. He was ready to inspect the breasts and perhaps a little more. His wife would never know. Perhaps this was God's way of paying him back for all his kindness towards her during her illness. He rang the front bell and spoke through the intercom to a liquid, deep, and sensual female voice that buzzed the main entrance's electronic lock open.

He knocked at the door of Eufemia's fifteenth-floor apartment at exactly 2:05 P.M. and was greeted by a tall, slender, graceful goddess in her early thirties. She was mesmerizing, more than he had ever expected. He was entranced by the quality of her bone structure, her exquisitely chiseled features reminiscent of the classic Maya, with large, upturned deep brown eyes and lustrous, long, blue-black hair worn in a loose, almost Roman fashion. She had the legs and hips of a young deer as she walked across the beautifully furnished living room in a pale gold silk dressing gown.

He sat down on the soft sofa and gazed up into the promised land. The breasts! Oh yes! They were beautiful, perfectly sized, rounded, pert, and firm, everything Chon had promised! Eufemia did a bit of her act for him, dancing in the silk dressing gown, hinting at revelation until he was practically beside himself.

"Chon has told me that you want to see my *tetas*," she said seductively.

The politico nodded eagerly, almost without control. "Si! Si!"

"Ask nicely," she teased him coyly.

"Si, por favor!" he begged.

Eufemia disrobed in one fluid stroke and was completely naked underneath the silky garment. She stood stately, revealing a slender body that appeared to have been blown of amber glass into a subtle, almost hourglass shape to hold the most exotic of all wines. The politico's eyes popped and his tongue wagged. "Ay Mamasita, mi diosa," he crooned.

She approached him. "Would you like to touch me?" she invited. "Touch them."

He reached out and felt her breasts, which were soft and supple to the touch. "Natural," he said. "They feel completely natural."

"Now touch my *cuca*," she bade him.

This was more than he could have hoped for. She was inviting him to caress her vagina.

"Does it feel natural?" she asked him as he stroked her.

"Oh yes!" he groaned. "Very natural."

It was obvious that he was extremely excited and had achieved a hard erection which she felt gently and approvingly with her hand. "Mmm! Chon will be glad to know that you were able to become so aroused."

"Make love with me," he pleaded.

"You make love to me," Eufemia responded as he rapidly removed his trousers. He was practically on top of her when she said, "Don't worry, querido, you will be able to please your wife like a macho. The same doctor who gave me my tetas also gave me my cuca, and look how hot you are. You take her to the best surgeons and you'll have no worries. Would you like the name of my doctor in Brazil?"

"What?" he gasped, dumbfounded.

Eufemia just smiled sweetly at him and repeated, "The doctor who gave me my cuca. You know!"

"Ay Dios mio!" the politician shouted as he struggled to get dressed. "That brujo bastard has made me worse than the stupidest cuckold with his tricks! I'll get him for this."

Don Juan howled with laughter. I heard cackling from the kitchen. The girls had been eavesdropping. We all broke into insane whoops and shouts.

Chon finished the story by saying that Eufemia then stood up defiantly, putting on her dressing gown. "You'll do nothing to Chon or I will announce to the Prensa that you were here wanting to make love with me today," she shouted.

Eufemia left the room and instructed her maid to politely show the man out after he had recovered himself. To hear Chon tell it, the politico showed up at the herb stand later that afternoon, almost at closing time, shouting "Tío Chon! Tío Chon!" *Tío* means uncle, but can sometimes be used as a derogatory familiar. "She has an artificial vagina, you disgraceful old wizard!" Chon smiled and told him that, based on Eufemia's comments, he would now be happy to include the blessing upon the artificial breasts in his wife's Primicia.

We couldn't take any more laughter. Our sides were splitting so that even doña Celestina was doubled over as she walked to the kitchen to ask the girls to clear the table. We retired to our rooms still snickering to ourselves and repeating lines from the story.

Chon's bedroom was the next one down the passage way from mine, with don Juan at the head of the passage on my other side. Doña Celestina had her bedroom off the consultation room, separated by a small hallway. This afforded her the facility of working on trabajitos late into the night, if she so desired. The sense of all of us under one roof was positively electric. My Dreaming was like a long cruise into pure energy.

The next day, rather than going to El Tecolote to trade herbs, Chon spent the entire time with the daughter of the woman who had come seeking doña Celestina's help the day before. He worked on the shy young girl in a vacant back room behind the patio, in the section of the house where the doña's girls slept. I could smell copal burning and knew that he was doing *limpias* and counseling her. This gave me time to converse with don Juan, since doña Celestina was now also occupied with trabajitos for her clients.

"Chon's story about Eufemia brings up a question, don Juan," I proposed.

"What question is that, muchacha mía?" he replied as he watered the papaya tree from a large tin bucket.

"After listening to Chon and Dreaming with all of you, I realize that sexual energy has much more to do with our lives than we are allowed to express in our conventional, repressed, modern culture."

"You're just now realizing that?" he joked.

"No, not really. But what can an ordinary person do to get out of all the traps, the repression, misuses, and abuses of our sexual energy that are condoned and promoted by society, by our religions, our values, our materialism, our own fears?"

"The first thing a person can do is not go crazy," he responded, putting down the bucket. "This is potent energy, a serious situation that requires sobriety. Let's sit down and we'll talk about it." We walked over to the nurturing and familiar rockers. "One thing that people have to do is to recapitulate the energy they have been given by their parents and ancestors, replete with all the powers, misconceptions, and misuses there may have been. They must evaluate how that energy was spent before conceiving them, what was its condition, and what portion of this was passed on to them, so that the blessings, imbalances, and depletions may be uncovered.

"Then they must look at how they have spent and possibly misused sexual energy themselves, with relation to themselves and their intendeds, in whatever configuration that may be. If they have children also, what portion of their dose of energy was passed on, and in what condition? In all these cases, once the nature of the beast has been carved out, it can be offered up to the flames, so to speak, disassembled, so that the energy may be called back at the proper moment, cleansed and in its rightful configuration.

"For example, I constantly see mothers and fathers who don't retrieve their energy from their children at the proper time. The portion of energy that a parent contributes is lent to the child, like support sticks that are placed around a seedling so that its trunk will grow to be straight. At the proper moment the parents may retrieve this energy, they must, in fact, otherwise the supports will cramp and possibly deform the growing offspring. What often happens instead is that parents fail, for whatever reasons, to remove their energy. This forces the young adult to carry a portion of the parental energy as a burden, for once adulthood is reached, a healthy human can be fully endowed with the energy allotted to it by creation.

"I even hear parents say 'I'll live forever in you, son, and in your children and in your children's children.' This makes the parents weak and clinging. Rightly speaking, they should live on, in themselves. This is an insidious tendency that creates both parents and children who are dependent. No one ever grows up and wants to change it. Everyone is a cripple by choice."

"Co-dependency is what psychologists now call what you are referring to," I mused.

"They say it but they don't See it, and that means they don't retrieve the energy. In so doing, one may find exquisite expressions for it. Ceremonies and acts of power may be undertaken to retrieve lost energy, but one must learn to acknowledge the value of that which is so naturally illuminating, and yet so hard won once lost.

"I can see now that each of us should share our own lessons with you while you are here. Perhaps our tales and practices will guide you in your own evolution and the quest for healing. I am certain that doña Celestina and Chon will be delighted to oblige. There is much to learn, much to express, Merlina. Life and death." He got up from his rocker and rubbed my head on the way to his room.

PRACTICE FIVE

RETRIEVING LOST ENERGY

1. Examine areas of your life where you invested energy that should have eventually been returned to you and was not. Examples might be a dysfunctional parent who continues to hold your energy in an abusive manner, or a child whom you cannot stop babying.
2. Perform a thorough recapitulation of the person or persons without informing them that you are doing so. (See Recapitulation, page 32.)
3. Intend a Dream in which, with a single act, you recover all lost or misplaced energy from said individual. Bridge some element of that act into the waking world. For example, if you Dream that you touch your father's left shoulder and your energy returns to you via the force of your intent, find some occasion to touch his shoulder in like manner, mindful of the silent power of intent, and feel that the act is completed.
4. Examine any behaviors of yours which encourage the individual to reactivate the pattern, and cease them. This will squeeze off the fibers that connect them to you in an undesirable way. The fibers will wither and the individual will be starved of the energy they were utilizing.

DRAWING AND
RELEASING ENERGY
IN NATURE

THE NEXT MORNING EVERYONE SEEMED TO BE AWARE of the game plan. Chon was up and waiting for me after I finished breakfast. "It seems that it's my turn today," he grinned. "I don't know when I'll get to El Tecolote. I may be here for days! Let's go take a ride in the desert and look at plants."

We walked behind doña Celestina's house to the area where I had parked the jeep and got into the front seats. Chon was carrying several collecting sacks in case he came across medicinal plants. He instructed me to drive east on a dirt road out of town that headed straight into the desert. We started off. Driving with Chon was new to me and very different from riding with don Juan. While don Juan was always serious while we were driving and frequently used the time for discussions, Chon on the other hand rode silently, and somehow there was a carnival-like atmosphere to his being a passenger. I found it difficult not to drift into reverie and felt as though we were floating off into the rising sun.

We stopped about fifteen miles outside of town in an area where there was definitely some underground water, judging by the mesquite trees and bushes. "I see some jojoba already," Chon said as he got out of the jeep.

When I stepped out on my side, the first plant I spied was an aggressively large jimson weed, also called the datura plant or *toloache,* growing not far from a mature, shady mesquite. The datura plant seemed to concentrate my attention. Despite my efforts to interest myself in the plants of the surrounding area, I kept returning my gaze to it.

"Toloache," Chon commented, pointing to the datura as he walked around to my side. "She likes you. Can't you smell her from here?"

I could in fact discern what I would have described as an itch in the air, seemingly coming from the breeze that blew directly behind the hardy plant.

"Let's walk over there," Chon suggested.

The plant was not in bloom and was wider and lower to the ground than a male plant would have been. The stalks were obscenely thick and covered with plentiful bunches of leaves and spiked round seed pods.

"Datura is really a woman's plant, so I'll begin with you here," Chon said. "A tea made from the leaves will bring a woman into heat, and a paste of the freshly ground leaves rubbed on the body will produce a flight of the energy body, often used by witches for pleasure, vision, and to strike at an enemy." Chon knelt down to show me a thick cluster of leaves. "The Maya smoke the leaves in a ceremony to divine or to Dream the location of lost persons or objects. We also drink a tea made of *calea zacatechichi,* which grows only in Chiapas, for the same purpose. In the ceremony, the entire community drinks the tea and enters into brief but intense periods of Dreaming induced by the plant, followed by involuntary awakenings, during which time we discuss the information we have brought back. When the H'men smokes datura leaves, it is done alone and during or following the smoke, or in Dreaming later, sight of that which is lost will come."

The shade of the mesquite tree became very inviting as its leaves rustled in the late autumn breeze. Chon and I both sensed this and, after sweeping two spots clear of leaves and rubble, we sat down underneath the tree with our backs against the trunk. "Nature is overflowing with vital and sexual energy and a practitioner can avail him- or herself of this by allying with elements of the natural world, elements such as wind, sun, water, earth, metal, stone, plant life, and creatures," Chon continued.

"There are infinite entry points in waking and Dreaming, everything from basic acts such as eating, drinking, breathing, walking, bathing, and sunning, to sophisticated supplications, invocations, and mergings practiced by shamans and healers. One way that a healer learns about the curative properties of plants, for example, is through Dreaming. Let's say that someone comes to me with an illness that I have never seen before and cannot cure at the time of their visit." Chon gives me a nudge. "I supplicate to the forces and spirits to show me a vision of the cure in Dreaming. If it takes the form of a plant with which I am not familiar, I must then bridge my Dreaming and go out into the world stalking the plant. I silence my mind and allow my energy body to guide me, pulling my physical body along as if by wires. I soften my gaze, enter into Dreaming awake by opening my Dream at the moment of the revelation, and just wander through the jungle or forest until I find the plant.

"When I find it, I express thankfulness and make a request of the plant's spirit, explaining my Dream and my search. Then in order to receive the methods of preparation and administration, I fall asleep at the site of the newly discovered plant and enter into Dreaming again with my intent. Once I have been blessed with all the knowledge I seek in Dreaming, I then awaken and ask permission of the plant to take some of it and prepare and administer it in the ways I have been shown.

"Upon returning to my home, I always place a portion of what I have taken on my altar, not to be used as medicine, but to be a representative portion of the plant entity to whom I wish to send blessings. I then instruct my patient in the ways they are to administer their cure according to what I have Dreamed. If they are very ill, I follow those instructions myself and administer the medicine along with any other treatments or ceremonies I may have Dreamed. Each night during the curing process I Dream the patient well and seek to open those Dreams with the patient each time we interact in the waking world."

Listening to the passionate, intimate nature with which Chon approaches healing, I understood why power had selected him as a natural healer. My eyes were moist when he finished talking. "I want you to try the same thing," he said as he got up from the ground, dusting off his backside. "This toloache has a message for you. While I scout around for other plants, I would like for you to fall asleep here under this kind tree, near the plant, and let her talk to you. See if she will share her strength with you. She is powerfully sexual, and a survivor. Remember, when making an ally, always share something in return."

Chon left me one of his sacks so that I might have a place to lay my head, and I curled up on my left side under the mesquite tree facing the plant as he walked away into the desert. I have never had any trouble falling asleep. Rather like a cat, I find that I can luxuriate in deep relaxation until it becomes ecstatic. Don Juan once remarked to me that felines are outstanding Dreamers who know how to draw energy from the sleep state. Unlike many creatures who awaken sluggishly, cats will sleep up to sixteen hours per day, and yet they are one of the most agile, supple, and powerful of all nature's creatures.

Within minutes I was snoozing pleasantly in the morning sun filtered by the overhanging branches of the large mesquite.

I Dreamed of yawning, awakening and opening my eyes to find that the large jimson weed was growing in my direction. The plant extended itself toward me and scuttled across the ground by sending out tentacle-like feelers covered with leaves that enveloped and eventually swallowed me.

I was moving through the interior of the plant, much like a whole egg moves through the body of a snake when swallowed. Green hemoglobin flowed around me and everything I saw filtered through a greenish hue. Deeper and deeper I went, being swallowed into the heart of the plant, the fragrance of weed and spice permeating the Dream.

When I arrived at the heart my legs became the roots, my arms the branches. A trumpeting white flower sprouted as my head and my ovaries turned in on themselves to become spiked, rounded seed pods. I spread like a starfish in five directions and felt a throbbing and pulsing as life force poured into my body. A sensation of warmth accompanied the feeling of flight and I could take in air as if my entire being had transformed into giant lungs. Fire from the molten earth began to flow in through my feet, the very tips of my roots, and my abdomen received a cool wellspring of water, drinking, gurgling, filling, and circulating the life-giving crystalline cleanliness.

The fragrance became known to me as my potency, my hypnotic state, my bewitching essence. I felt this as I became one with the plant, truly became its entirety and I remembered Chon's words, that I should give something in return. It was a difficult task, for I had come naked, with nothing, and then I thought "a song! Yes!" The stamen of my flowery head became my golden tongue and I sang as sweetly as ever I've sung in my life.

The words were unknown syllables filled with tone and vibration, the melody haunting and evocative. I began to awaken as I sang. Chon was sitting beside me under the mesquite tree with a full sack of plants. "Nice singing," he commented to me and rubbed my head.

I was drifting in and out, as if reminiscing a romance, as we walked to the jeep and started the slow drive back through the desert along the dirt road. "You should keep that song," Chon finally said. "Always sing it to toloache when you need to elicit her favors or when you wish to empower her effects. Just as you merged with her, so may you merge with other elements of nature if they allow it. It is important to always receive an invitation first, or to ask permission and receive it. This is foremost. Many clumsy seekers think that they can go in anywhere without requesting permission. They get punished for it. Never do such a thing. There is no romance or respect in it. It costs nothing to ask permission first, and there is everything to gain."

When we were about half of the way along, Chon spied a group of boulders that also seemed most inviting, and again he instructed me to stop the jeep. We got out and walked towards them, this time leaving the plant sacks behind in the locked vehicle. The outcropping was a rather phallic grouping of smooth standing stones. One had fallen on top of several others, creating an overhang, an enclosed rock shelter of sorts.

Before we proceeded any closer, Chon instructed me to feel for permission to approach and possibly enter the enclosure. A response came as a wave of pleasant, nurturing feelings. Chon said that if the site had refused, perhaps I might have felt a sense of revulsion and eerie mystery, or perhaps a sensation of uncleanliness. We entered through a space between two of the standing stones, which formed an irregular circle topped by the fallen stone, and found that the ceiling stone was a panel of rock art. Shaman figures, rattlesnakes, deer, and even a bighorn sheep scurried and danced happily across its surface.

"Judging by the shape of this structure and the picto-graphs," Chon began as we seated ourselves within, "this seems to have been a vision quest site. I'm sure Juan would agree. In fact, he probably knows about its historical use. What I can tell you is that spots like this were used in cere-mony when a particular practitioner would isolate him- or herself and seek to merge with the rock, to go within it and learn from the spirit inside. Often, as well, the spirit was enticed to come out. This ceiling panel here," he said, pointing above our heads, "was a kind of Stone Age cinema. The seeker would lie or sit back and gaze into the surface of the rock with a soft focus and a silent mind. The isolation would let the world stop and through serious gazing and unbending intent, the practitioner's attention would shift to the life within the rock. This was done easily by those who never made the mis-take of seeing stones and mountains as dead matter.

"Rocks, crevices and caves are portals into other realms of Earth, and mountains are the abodes of spirits. Lizards like this little fellow here are the go-betweens of the realms." A small chuckwalla stopped and peered at us before racing across the earthen floor and into a crevice between two of the stones. "Snakes, as I know Juan has told you, are the guardians. Males seek to enter into the rock in feminine places and then go toward the masculine, hence this womblike enclo-sure on the inside, formed by erect stones on the outside.

"The Maya have similar initiation chambers in under-ground caverns. The cave and the water flowing within her are the feminine properties, as well as the snake guardians within. The rock surfaces and the fire a shaman brings with him are the masculine, although the fire beneath the Earth is female. Together they can make steam, life, gold. For a male, vision questing within stone is like ritual lovemaking. For a female it is like being made love to. Lie back here and see what I mean."

I lay back and gazed up at the ceiling panel which seemed illuminated in places by a play of sunlight upon different minerals within it and upon small pock marks and irregularities of its surface, to give the impression of a sky filled with stars. The shaman figures were lively, all carrying sticks or lightning spears, seemingly ready for diminutive intercourse with the cosmos, the rock, the sky, the clouds for rain. There was something thrilling and erotic about the dance of figures on the panel and as I lay there I felt titillated, joyful, and even wanted to laugh joyfully, as though I were being tickled or flirted with. I could easily envision that in Dreaming these sensations could flower into full-fledged ecstasy.

"See what I mean?" Chon whispered, smiling.

"Potent little guys," I responded.

"Potent energy," Chon replied.

"I get the impression that making rain was like the sky having an orgasm," I mused.

"Out here in the middle of the desert, you'd better believe it!" Chon cheered gleefully.

We both laughed and sat up with our backs against a stone. What a wonderful spot! I felt fantastic. Not only had I been protected, replenished, and nurtured by the powers there, but also flirted with! I resolved to come back one day on my own and sleep there.

PRACTICE SIX

DRAWING AND RELEASING ENERGY IN NATURE

1. Select a sunny spot, perhaps a smooth boulder or a grassy area near flowing water. Lie upon the spot face down and completely relax. Breathe out all the toxic energy by exhaling with a soft moan, pushing the abdomen in on the exhale. Feel all the heavy, tired, diseased energy drain into the Earth to be recycled. If flowing water is nearby, allow the sensation of its flowing to wash through you, positioning yourself so the flow moves from your feet, through your body, to your head and beyond. Release the toxic energy with the same moaning exhale and abdominal push.

2. Fall asleep for a moment and allow the process to continue in Dreaming, releasing the energy even more fully.

3. Roll over onto your back and allow the sunlight to renew every aspect of your being. Take sunlight into the eyes through barely parted lids, using your lashes to soften the light. Allow the Earth to recharge your spinal column with sturdy fire energy. Breathe in and expand your abdomen on the inhale, feeling the support of the Earth.

4. Fall asleep again and continue the renewal process in Dreaming, drinking the sunlight energy into your Dream and your luminous awareness.

5. Awaken and thank the spot. Revive, stand, and stretch, breathing deeply.

SHAPESHIFTER
DREAMING

THE RUNNING JOKE IN THE HOUSE BECAME WHOSE turn it was for the day, and the following day it was don Juan's. The sorcerers did not follow a turnabout order, but rather a topical one which might involve several repeating turns or the skipping of someone, and so no predictable pattern could be theorized by me and I was constantly in a state of delightful surprise.

My lesson began with a morning walk in the desert and a search for rattlesnakes. Don Juan assured me they had plenty to tell. We trod carefully in a dry water canyon, checking crevices and under rocks as we passed. Don Juan carried a long stick forked at the tip, with which he could pin a rattler's head if need be. Finally, as we neared a turn, we spied a baby rattlesnake hiding in a high crevice above a boulder at about shoulder height. We inched closer and it began to hiss and rattle, rearing and offering a few mock strikes.

"Is the mother near by?" I asked, concerned.

"Not likely," don Juan responded. "Once babies like this little guy here are born, the mother leaves them to fend for themselves. That's why they're so nasty." The tiny rattler hissed emphatically. "Rattlers give birth to live young, unlike some snakes which lay eggs, a rattler's favorite food. To protect her offspring, a mother gives them one gift, a bite as strong and venomous as her own, although the babies are puny by comparison. Other creatures know this and leave them alone. If you were to try to handle this fellow, you'd most likely get quite a dose of its venom. Once they mature a bit, they learn not to waste their toxin on creatures too large for them to eat and will frequently 'dry bite' a large aggressor in order to save their lethal charge for a small mammal, reptile or bird."

"That's quite intelligent," I remarked as the baby rattler turned to face the noisemaker and offered a mock strike in my direction.

"Since shamans saw rattlers as pure sexual energy, the desert cultures around this area learned from the lesson. The men especially learned about the conservation of this energy and about its potency, which resulted in very long-lived, tall men, as you know. The women learned about its concentrated potency and miraculous abundance, which made the women wise and the children strong. We did not overpopulate the area, since the desert was our teacher, and yet there was no lack of passion. Let's move on and let this little fellow relax. We'll find a spot to sit and talk around the bend."

We proceeded, much to the baby rattler's relief, and did in fact find a shady spot under some overhanging rock, which was, upon close inspection, entirely free of snakes, scorpions and insects. We brushed the ground clean and sat down to relax, shielded from the steadily rising sun. I pulled out a water bottle from my pack and offered don Juan a drink before taking one myself.

"Besides observing rattlesnakes, what other methods were employed to learn from them?" I asked curiously once we were settled.

"As Chon has already told you, permission must be asked and obtained before one may begin. The process is one of Dreaming and bridging. In the first step, the Dreams are of snakes. One may Dream of seeing snakes or, as you have done, one may actually Dream of talking with them."

I vividly recalled the Dream to which he referred. He had left me Dreaming on a rock by a cool stream and, shortly afterwards, a rattlesnake had appeared in the Dream and had spoken with me at length. I then told don Juan that I had finally bridged that Dream into the waking world and he urged me to recount the entire experience.

"Well," I began, "I was walking in the mountains above Tucson on a cool stormy night, not long after returning from Mexico. I had my flashlight with me. It was a beautiful night filled with strong breezes, lightning and a soft rain. As I neared a curve on the dirt foot path, I spied a rattlesnake stretched full length across it, cooling its underbelly on the moistened earth. I shone the light from my flashlight across the length of the snake and could perceive that there were bushes on either side of the path, so there was no way to step around it. The sudden light seemed not to irritate it. It rather seemed to bask in the light. The snake neither hissed, nor rattled, nor coiled and made no motion to strike or to slither away. I could perceive from the light reflected in its eye that it was alive, fully awake, and aware of my presence, however it did not seem in the least apprehensive. Rather, it was sublimely relaxed, almost hypnotic."

"A snake cannot strike when it's stretched straight. It must coil to strike, but that's not the important point. Go on," don Juan urged.

"I pondered what to do, whether I should wait or turn back. The presence of a large rattler so close to me was stunning and I found myself being very still and respectful, not making any unnecessary movements. The thought even occurred to me that the snake seemed so relaxed I might step across its length softly and proceed with my walk, to which I heard a startling reply."

Don Juan laughed out loud. "That snake crossed your path in the most dramatic way possible," he said emphatically, pointing his index finger at me. "He did it literally and with full awareness. It was an appointment with power. There was no way that you were going anywhere else. To have behaved carelessly would have been the terribly dangerous waste of a gift."

"That is exactly what the snake told me!" I shouted, astonished, silently realizing how silly I might sound out of context. "Its eye peered directly into mine and I heard with my ears and with the center of my forehead. It said, 'I know you're not going to take another step.'"

"What did you learn?" don Juan asked with keen interest.

"The snake showed me how it can make a staff of itself, how to produce deep trance and relaxation, how to rest for well-being, and how to be in heightened awareness simultaneously. I also learned that snakes can be friendly and fearless, but that they are never foolhardy. I felt awe for their wisdom and I also perceived that they know the exact moment when energy is being taxed or patience is strained. I felt compelled to back away respectfully at that precise moment, and I did not turn my back to the rattler until I had walked backwards to round the bend again."

"I applaud your achievement," don Juan said sincerely. "It's time for you to learn the next step in the process, which is to become snake. Let's go back and see our little friend again. I'm sure he's still around."

We got up, dusted ourselves off and walked a short distance back to the place in the canyon where we had seen the baby rattler earlier. Peeking into the crevice, I could see that it was still there, almost unchanged in location. It hissed at me as if to remind me of its previous warning, but did not move to rear or strike as long as I did not make any false moves.

Don Juan came closer, opened a pouch tied to his trousers and handed me a small nest of twigs that he had fashioned himself that morning before I had awakened. Next he handed me a preserved quail egg that he had obtained from doña Celestina. He instructed me to place the egg within the nest, not far, but at a non-threatening distance from the small rattlesnake. We then took a walk in the desert for about an hour and a half, following which we retraced our steps.

Upon returning to the snake's crevice in the canyon, I was not surprised to find that the nest was empty. The little serpent's face revealed no secret other than satisfaction, but there was a guilty lump not far behind his mouth.

"It will take him a while to digest the egg," don Juan commented. "Gradually the bulge will move back through his body and get smaller and smaller. There'll be no solid waste, for snakes have perfect digestion," he explained.

We walked on to the shady overhang where we had rested earlier and again seated ourselves. "The next step in Dreaming is to become snake," don Juan continued. "Often one Dreams that one is bitten first, but in your case, I don't think this is necessary. You now have an affinity with rattlers. I know from working with Chon the Maya Dream of being swallowed by a large serpent. If the tail goes up and the head comes down from the cosmos, they ascend into higher realms of energy. If the tail points down and the head rises from the underworld, they descend into the lower realms called Xibalba. The Yuman practice is to Dream into the spine in order to transform into snake. You may try whichever you prefer, or both. Let power decide which is right for you, and the order in which to proceed. Why don't you make yourself comfortable here and Dream? The well-fed little rattler not far from here will surely come to your assistance. I'll walk on a ways and see what else is happening in the desert this afternoon. Later I'll come back for you and we can drive into San Luis for a bite of lunch."

Don Juan got up and continued his walk through the canyon. His strategies were always flawless. By leaving me right around lunch time, I had nothing to do but think about my growing appetite and impatiently await his return, or disregard it and patiently sleep while he enjoyed his walk. Motivated by curiosity and common sense, I opted for the latter.

Leaning my back against a boulder in the shade of an overhanging rock, I found that I was soon dozing and that my attention, by virtue of the pressure exerted by the boulder, was centered within my spine. It wasn't long before I perceived a golden energy concentrated there, which floated like liquid mercury within a staff-like column. I entered Dreaming and swam energetically down to the base of it, where I merged with this golden, liquid life and instantaneously I awakened within it, which caused it to rise straight up and fountain out the top of my head, much like the hooded king cobra.

The crowning point of this energy then bowed itself slightly forward so that it faced frontally and a single eye appeared therein which opened by separating lids and then again by lifting or rolling back a translucent hood from the eye. Below the tip of the eye the golden energy coned and there formed a tongue and a mouth, as if to speak wisdom and to sing, and the entire Dream vibrated like harp strings in the wind.

Then my Dreaming awareness was swallowed by this golden serpent and I found myself fully awakened in the waking world without any loss of heightened awareness, or memory of the experience. I heard don Juan's light tread on the desert gravel about 100 yards away. He was beaming, a broad smile across his face.

"I know you're famished," he said enthusiastically, slapping my back as I rose eagerly from the spot. I dusted myself off and scrambled to keep up with his pace. He was right. "Let's see what we can get in San Luis that will match that appetite of yours!"

On the way to the jeep we paid a respectful visit of thanks to the baby rattler, still in his crevice and happily digesting his quail egg. Don Juan retrieved the little nest of twigs that he had made and we cheerily trudged on.

Once inside the jeep and on the road back to town, it was obvious that even don Juan was eager to discuss the afternoon's Dream, but only in the company of good and plentiful food. We stopped at one of his favorite places, a nondescript restaurant with no name painted above the entrance. It had a large back room filled with tables under ceiling fans, around a blackboard listing the day's bountiful selections.

We ordered sparkling mineral water with limes, meatball soup, cheese enchiladas, and chile rellenos with corn tortillas. Don Juan rubbed his hands eagerly over the steaming tortilla basket, opening the soft cloth to reveal freshly made tortillas, and offered me one. The waitress placed our water with limes and bowls of soup, along with freshly chopped jalapeños, on the red-and-white checkered tablecloth and left us to enjoy, saying "Buen provecho."

Don Juan rolled a tortilla and dunked it in the savory soup. "Was Dreaming snake what you expected?" he asked with a grin.

"Not at all," I said quietly. "I don't know what I preconceived, but that certainly wasn't it. The experience was so much more esoteric, much more exotic than I had anticipated. Sensual. I'm reminded of ancient Egyptian Pharaohnic headdresses and tales of yogis from India."

Don Juan gave me a questioning glance.

"What I mean to say is that both those cultures seem to describe something similar or allude to the experience I just had. They placed a great deal of stock in it. Now I can see that without having the experience, no one can truly understand what they were talking about, and yet the fact that they seem to concur pales to the experience itself."

Don Juan questioned me about the headdresses and the Egyptian penchant for pyramid building, which he compared to the Maya. "The realizations are not quite the same," he commented. "The focus is different, but they were seeing something not unlike what shamans have seen for millennia. Perhaps another difference is the way the knowledge was put to use. Since their serpents were golden as yours, I will tell you that gold is not the final form of the serpent, you know. How few people ever get far enough to see that! The qualities of gold are incorruptibility and that it can withstand a good burn. No matter what you defile it with, fire of sufficient intensity will separate the gold and restore its purity, which does not char or mar under any circumstances. That is quite an energetic accomplishment, and yet gold can be heavy for some, though I think that this is not so in your case. The serpent can transform still further, however."

"Into what?" I gasped, totally enthralled.

"Ah! Now that is the great mystery," he responded softly, almost at a whisper.

"Rainbows! Light." I whispered in realization, even more softly. "You will tell me more, don Juan, won't you?"

"That is one reason I called you back here, Merlina. I'm getting to be an old snake whose venom has been fermenting like a cactus wine for a long time. If done right, aging makes the energetic wine grow stronger and more concentrated. This last shedding of skin will be more like a cocoon for me."

I shuddered. Don Juan was speaking of things I was not quite ready to face, and yet from his expression I could see that the moment was not far off.

PRACTICE SEVEN

SHAPESHIFTER DREAMING

1. Begin by gazing at the desired creature in Dreaming, be it serpent, hawk, even tree. Ask permission to join with it and focus your gaze into the eyes, or the essence, viewing the remainder of the creature with your peripheral vision. Feel the energy reciprocating.
2. Slowly dissolve the barrier between the "me" that is Dreaming you and the "me" that is Dreaming the creature.
3. Allow your energy body to travel, to zoom in, becoming more and more of the desired form as it moves forward.
4. Share peacefully with the awareness already present there, the body and perceptions into which you have shifted.
5. Explore your Dreaming domain for the length of time your energy will allow, remembering that when you run out of energy for Dreaming, it ends.
6. There is no need to Dream that you return to your normal form. This will occur naturally when your energy for Dreaming is used up. You will awaken from Dreaming with fresh knowledge and perceptions for both your physical and energy bodies.

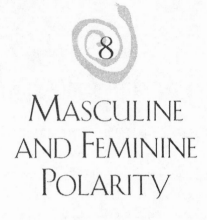

MASCULINE
AND FEMININE
POLARITY

AT 4:00 A.M. THE FOLLOWING MORNING, I WAS SUMMONED
into doña Celestina's altar room by Neida's knock
and a whisper at my door. I fumbled in the dark for matches to
light a candle, smoothed my hair and splashed my face, slipped
on a simple cotton dress, and made my way under starlight
through the passageway. I knew from prior experiences with
doña Celestina that she expected one to be presentable and
ready to work whenever she chose, and I would never have
considered taking a moment longer to present myself. An insis-
tent knock in the early hours is always unsettling and com-
pelling, demanding immediate alertness. My stays with Chon
had taught me to be prepared, as these stays were often simi-
larly interrupted by urgent healing calls, at any hour of the day
or night. I adjusted to being startled, knowing that this was
part of the work. After drawing a long, deep breath, I tapped
at the altar room door and heard doña Celestina's voice tell me
to come in.

The room was lit by the flame of one white candle which
burned on the altar table. A window was partially open to the
night air and a soft breeze blew the curtain gently. Doña
Celestina was dressed in black and seated behind the altar.
There was a vacant chair in front of the altar, facing her. She

motioned for me to be seated there. As I did so, I took stock of the wide array of ritual items that had been placed on the table, which seemed to be the reason for the call, or the focus of our work.

"These hours are the best for the kind of work I often do," doña Celestina began, by way of an explanation. "Energetically, at this time of night people are quite susceptible to influences in Dreaming. Between 2:00 and 4:00 in the morning is the time when sorcerers leap and when most possession and other dark works are done. One should be aware of this in order to effect the antidotes. Tonight I have been working on the stepfather of that young, victimized girl, whose mother you met in my consultation. Would you like to ask me about possession and my work with that man, or why I have called you in?"

Her tone was so somber and businesslike that it was evident she had just completed a long work session. "You've told me before that there are several types of possession. How do they relate to what you are doing for that young woman and her mother?" I asked with caution. "And what does this work have to do with why you have called me here?"

"Good. There are many kinds of possession, Merlina. Some involve removing the energy body of an individual from the physical body and keeping it for a time, temporarily borrowing it in order to do work, either for good or bad. During sleep the energy body journeys anyway, sometimes receiving night lessons, so this makes the work easy. There are positive and negative possessions, you see. Most people, even those who say they know about witchcraft, are unaware of this. For example, a person who cannot fight a force in their lives, like the unfortunate young girl or her mother, may actually request a positive possession. In that case, they are asking to be bound in protection. Most types of possession always involve binding or containment. First you must bring the energy body to you, or leap towards it. Then you may affect it, teach it, bind, or hold it. Shamans, sorcerers, long-distance healers, spirits, even celestial beings seemingly all use this method. A scrupulous energy will later return what has been borrowed, after the work that has been requisitioned is completed. An unscrupulous one will often try to find a way not to do so.

"Another type of possession is that of controlling the energetic and physical bodies of the intended. There are many levels of this, ranging from the temporary possession of mediums by discarnate or carnate entities, to full-fledged occupation. These techniques were discovered first by shifters. I know that Juan worked with you yesterday on this practice. Once an energetic rapport has been established, once you can reconfigure your energy body into another energetic form, a being that dwells in that form may invite you to share bodies. So in the case of a crow, for example, one must first go through the process of being able to transform one's own energy body into that of crow. At that point, one may communicate with crow and one possibly may be invited to leap, to exit one's own body energetically and temporarily share the body of crow for the mutual benefit of both. The crow learns from the practitioner and the practitioner learns from crow.

"Naturally, you can see how the possibility for abuse arises once practitioners latch on to the energetic interconnectedness of shifting. Some proceed correctly, with impeccable intent, permission and invitation. Others manipulate the energy. As a result, the practices have been guarded and kept secret. What I have been doing with the abusive stepfather of that young girl is to temporarily borrow him at night, to bring him here and teach him lessons that affect his will to engage in the kind of behavior that has almost ruined his stepdaughter's life. Fear is a great teacher.

"I've called you in, Merlina, because I saw upon completing my work for this night that there is a great lesson for you here in male and female energy. I've set up my altar with everything I'll need to teach it to you. I've given Chon and Juan a task today to run an errand for me so that we will not be affected by their presence until you've seen what I have to show you."

I heard the sound of the front gate being closed. "They'll be gone now, so you can go have a shower and some breakfast. Meet me back here after the sun has come up."

In a daze, I went back to my room to get my shower supplies. I couldn't decide who was the greater task master. Each of my three mentors had a way of naturally demanding more of me than I would have thought possible, and of behaving as though it were all effortless. And yet, in shifting my level of awareness to accommodate each of them, their tasks truly became pleasurable and I could sense, through my level of well-being, that something was happening.

I returned to the altar room after refreshing myself and breakfasting alone on chicken tamales, eggs, and strong coffee in the kitchen. The patio had a much more graceful feeling with almost everyone out of the house. It seemed now to be the domain proper of morning sunlight, which caressed the space. I waited in a chair outside the altar room until doña Celestina appeared in the passageway and opened the door for us to enter.

Inside the morning light was streaming through the open window, something I had never seen, since the room was always kept dark with heavy closed curtains. I had my first real opportunity to look around. Outside the window I could see that there was a small, private garden area for doña Celestina's special hexing, antidote, and medicinal plants. The entire length of the three walls nearest it, which were of a pale earthen hue, was lined with old wooden cabinets, shelves and niches, which gave the impression of an apothecary. All the cabinets were kept neatly closed. On the final wall, to the right of the entrance, stood a large floor mirror on a pedestal, covered by a black sheet, and a row of six straight-backed wooden chairs. The altar table was placed at an angle slightly facing the entrance and occupied an off-center location near the middle of the room. An overall warmth shone from the fired terra-cotta floor tiles, and the ceiling, which was white, had dark, heavy wooden support beams running across its length.

The altar was covered with ritual objects just as I had seen it earlier. Doña Celestina seated herself and again motioned for me to sit across from her at the table.

"This lesson is about the power of complete woman and who possesses it," she stated in a serious and emphatic tone. "The items you see here are representatives of the many powers she wields. I want you to first gaze at the 'mesa,' her word for an empowered work of ritual placed upon an altar, and tell me if you feel or sense that there are any of these powers missing within you." She commanded me with her eyes to fix my gaze upon the array in silence.

I carefully examined every item in an attempt to comprehend the relevance of each to female power. Also, I gazed upon the holistic presentation for the total effect. In the center of the mesa sat a clay bowl filled with water and small orange flowers. A ripened pomegranate was placed behind the bowl, and a large hunting knife sat to the right of it. A clay chalice occupied a place to the upper left of the bowl. Within the chalice there was water and a heart-shaped, polished clear quartz stone. Below the chalice sat a long, clear quartz crystal wand, perfect in its natural unpolished state. Above all of these items, and laid across the width of the mesa, was a rain stick made from a dried shaft of organ pipe cactus. A large, spiraling cone shell placed point up, above and perpendicular to the center of the rain stick, occupied the uppermost position on the mesa.

The total effect was quite enthralling, and while I had to admit that I did not yet understand the significance of every piece placed on the mesa, I intuitively felt, internally scanning my body with a sense of my own energy, that I was not missing anything represented as a female power there. I asserted this to doña Celestina.

"You're right," she said, relieved, as though she had perhaps been uncertain that I would be able to come to this determination on my own. "That's what makes you such a desirable candidate for this work. That's why we were all drawn to you, each in our own way. However, the world is such that even a woman in your position, with whole power, may not realize that fact. For most women, the story is quite different. In addition to the world we live in, most women are missing one or more powers from the mesa. So the lesson I have for you today is for all women, and even for men. I suggest you find some way later on to share it."

"Would you please explain, doña Celestina, what you see each of the powers to be and how they can be lost?"

"I intend to do much more than that," she acknowledged. "I will also tell you how the powers can be retrieved, for that is the task I give to many women in order to help them. Some of the powers you will know yourself. Some may come as a surprise to you. The centerpiece is the womb," she said, turning the clay bowl counter-clockwise with the index finger of her left hand, "made from earth, and yet there is a celestial womb as well, which is also feminine," she indicated the celestial womb, or zenith, the center of creation directly above us, with the same finger.

"I have heard dreary stories from some of my Catholic clients that the church tells women they come from a rib of the first man. Have you ever once seen that?" she went on.

I had to laugh.

"I'm glad you see the humor in it. Many women do not," the doña continued. "The flowers floating inside represent the ability to open. The water is the orgasmic response. Look how full the bowl is. Many women have a cracked or an empty bowl which means that through some means, they have lost their capacity for orgasm. I like to compare this earthly condition to the rise of the Aztecs. When they arrived at the sacred lake of their dream-visions, they drained it so that they might build their capital upon the dry bed. The bed was on a fault, a crack between several different realms of earthly creation, and when they drained it and put undue pressure of the wrong kind upon it, it became unstable. The Aztec people lost certain healing, feminine, saving graces and became sacrificial and warlike. They believed that if they returned blood for the water they had stolen, the earth would not quake and destroy their world. Such is the fate of many women today who have been treated abusively in the extreme. Very little good can come of it."

"What can women do to take responsibility for the situation, rather than acting like victims?" I asked, very concerned.

"The first task is very basic. Women must recover their orgasms, any way they can," she replied bluntly.

My mind wandered across myriad possibilities. Doña Celestina softly nudged me under the table with her foot. "Paints quite a picture, doesn't it?" she smirked. "The power of the womb has been severely neglected in favor of that of the vagina."

"Pussy power," I thought to myself, and couldn't help but break into laughter which was evidently what she had intended.

She also burst out laughing. "Laughter has power," she finally said. "It's healthy. Women are not going to recover their missing energy by being morose."

I thought of making a checklist numbered in order of necessity. Number one: Orgasms. What a place to begin!

"That's the beginning," she reaffirmed. "The womb is the first brain and men don't have one. It's important to remember that. It fills with water from the orgasmic response." She lifted the rain stick erect, that caused it to emit beautiful, rain-falling sound upon both of us, as corn kernels fell through the labyrinth of thorns that had been pushed from the exterior of the staff through to the interior of it in order to lengthen the fall. "We'll talk about that more later. Another of the feminine powers is her seed," she said, pointing to the pomegranate. "They are whole within themselves and can make other whole females, but they can also change by themselves to make a male if need be. There are plants and reptiles which can do this. Hence the shamanic emphasis on these species. The male then can be a strategic variant to enhance the whole, which is both male and female simultaneously. See?"

"I do see!" I said, astounded. I almost couldn't believe what I was hearing! Finally someone knew what was never expressed and was explaining it, and not only that, doña Celestina lived it!

"Now the other pieces on the altar will become clear," she continued. "The knife is woman's ferocious edge to defend her young. If you don't believe she has one, just try getting between a mother bear and her cub. She will fight to preserve her life so that she may care for the offspring, and at the same time will fight to the death to keep anything from doing harm to her young. Many human females have abdicated their edge because they are afraid of it. It's very sharp and dangerous, and in fear they bestow it upon the males. The edge can be dulled though, through successive childbearing if the woman is unwilling to stand up for them. And sometimes it is against males who wield her borrowed edge that she must defend herself and her young.

"Woman is by no ways obligated to bear children, although most are told differently. She may use her edge to preserve herself." Doña Celestina picked up the hunting knife and brandished it at me with a ferocious glint in her eye. I recoiled slightly.

"Males have become interested in something besides our edge. And that brings me to this," she said, and picked up the crystal wand.

"Women have a phallic energy within them. Inside," she repeated, pointing to the area below her womb. "They must have it in order to produce good quality male offspring if need be. Men are attracted to it, as it enhances their own maleness and, over the centuries, we have played the old 'I've got your nose' game." She referred to the trick of pinching a child's nose and then showing them a portion of the thumb between the first and second fingers of the offending hand, saying "I've got your nose!"

"If you believe that someone has taken something from you, even if that is not possible, you will empower the illusion," she continued. "They may then borrow what they desire for an indefinite time. Have you ever loaned someone something and had them fail to return it?"

I nodded.

"And then when you finally go to them and ask for its return, they deny ever having had it?" she challenged.

"Yes, I have," I answered truthfully.

"Well, that is the plight of a disempowered woman and that's exactly where a witch comes in." She smiled with a cold glint in her eyes and teeth.

I sat back and drew a deep breath. The scope of her analysis was quite beyond anything I had anticipated, and so right on the money that it caused me pause.

"Men don't need to borrow that which we have already given them by grace. That's the easy way for indolent males. It's important to remember that we give them phallic energy by reproducing, not by giving away our own!"

"Good God," I exclaimed.

"Exactly," doña Celestina seconded. "Now this horn here," she said, picking up the large cone shell, "I'm going to let Juan talk to you about this. Not because I cannot, but because this is his condition energetically at this time."

"What about the chalice?" I asked.

"Ah, that is a great mystery," doña Celestina replied. "Another lake, Merlina, like that of the womb. Only this one is in the heart. It is a spirit lake." She whispered the words "spirit lake."

PRACTICE EIGHT

THE MESA (ALTAR)

1. To prepare a mesa for ritual purification and empowerment, you first need to find a sacred space within your home that is private and lends itself to ceremonial work. You will need a table, an empty chest, or an alcove with a shelf.
2. Select a cloth, either of a woven design or of a single color, to cover the working plane of your table, chest, or shelf. You may choose to melt the wax of multi-colored candles over your working plane, creating a solid wax surface upon which to do work, rather than covering the area with a cloth.
3. Select items to represent all of the powers of a complete womb. These items should include the waters of the womb, the wand or phallic energy, the edge, the flowering principle, the earthen vessel representing the womb space and the blood, and fire in the form of a candle.
4. Meditate upon the mesa and try to sense if any of the powers represented there are missing within you. Males, for example, often do not know how to find their womb space. Women, conversely, have often given away their phallic energy, sometimes unbeknownst to themselves.
5. Meditate upon the mesa to discern any imbalances, areas of depletion or over-emphasis. Search for areas that seem angry, damaged, or energetically unclean. Follow this with recapitulation. (See Recapitulation, page 32.)
6. Purify your entire mesa with the smoke of burning copal, the most neutral and powerful cleansing spirit within smoke. Leave the set-up mesa well protected, as you will return to it often for further work.

CULTIVATING
THE SEXUAL
ENERGY

AS DOÑA CELESTINA HAD INDICATED, DON JUAN WAS waiting for me the next morning, chipper and back from his mysterious errand with no mention of what he and Chon had been up to. "Doña Celestina told me that she left an item on the mesa for me to talk with you about," don Juan said after we had finished breakfast. "I will tell you about it, but not today. We have some work to do before we can speak of this."

"Are we going somewhere today, don Juan?"

"Yes, I think I'll have you drive us to a little park I know, near the center of San Luis. There are old eucalyptus and nice benches for sitting and watching the passersby. Doña Celestina has a friend who owns a very good Chinese restaurant close to the park. She recommends that we try it, and so we can make a day of it."

There was no sign of Chon anywhere in the house. After getting my handbag from my room, don Juan and I set out in the jeep towards the town center. He was right. The park was lovely and already filled with morning life. Surrounded by tall eucalyptus, the small square had a lush green lawn with a fountain and gazebo at the center. Sidewalks edged the little park and crisscrossed its center, creating a promenade for young girls with their mothers to stroll about. Wrought iron benches lined the perimeter underneath the eucalyptus and provided a place for adolescent boys and older men to sit and watch the strolling women.

We found a solitary bench under a thick, leafy eucalyptus and sat down comfortably. Several Cocopa and Mexican gentlemen sat on some of the other benches, snoozing under their straw hats or relaxing and gazing at the sway of the trees. It was a clear, mild, sunny day, perfect for being outside. A shoeshine stand had been set up on one corner and, not far from there, a newspaper vendor was displaying the second shipment of his morning array. Across the way, a woman was selling freshly squeezed orange juice; in an hour or two musicians would arrive. Ah, the pace of life in Mexico!

Don Juan settled back and stretched his legs. I did the same. The fresh breeze and the rustle of eucalyptus combined with a chorus of grackles to create a sensation that was sublime. "While we relax and enjoy, I want to take the opportunity to show you a special breath," he said. "Chon uses a similar breath in his healing work. I know you have heard him use it when he's doing an energetic healing."

"Yes! I was hoping someone would show me that breath in more detail!" I encouraged him. "Chon calls it a fire breath."

"That's a good name, for lack of a better one," don Juan agreed. "Sit up straight, stretch your back, relax and breathe in from your nostrils, pulling up gently on all the muscles of your lower body, every one. Plant your feet firmly on the ground and, when you breathe in, contract your abdomen. This creates a sensation of heat, like a bellows fueling a fire. Keep breathing this way until you have pulled the heat up into the back of your abdomen. Then, continuing the breath, pull the heat into your heart, then to the back of your throat, up to the back sinuses, the back of your head, and then to the top. The heat comes up the back, see?"

I tried the breath, following his demonstration, and I was amazed at the sensation of heat that welled up within my body. It rose up my back as he had said, and as it did my hands became tingly and began to perspire. They felt magnetized. My skin was slightly moist all over.

"That's good," he said. "Now let the sensation drip down from the top of your head into the center of your forehead. This is the liquid side, where all the fluids move. The heat will feel thick, moist. Swallow it as it drips down from your forehead and then feel it coat your throat, melt into the front of your heart, and radiate into your lungs. As you breathe down the front, inhale the warm steam. Expand your abdomen on the inhale. Increase its size to collect and fill with the liquid heat, like a pool. When you inhale, relax and expand the way a baby does when it breathes, the way a puma or jaguar breathes when it growls. Let the warm liquid energy flow into your sides, fill the organs there, and then drip down into your womb, the sexual organs. Collect and hold the energy in the center of will, the umbilical region, right behind and slightly below the navel, and feel it spin as it twists and concentrates into powerful intent, life-giving force."

I followed his instructions precisely. It felt as though someone had poured large amounts of warm honey through a hole in the center of my head when I breathed in deeply and expanded my abdomen. The warmth dripped, flowed, and melted down the front of my body, causing my eyes to moisten, my throat to swallow involuntarily, and my heart to ooze an emotion that felt very like love, which then spread warmth into my lungs and flowed to both arms and hands, causing a gentle, caressing sensation. My sides filled with vital energy and I actually felt the energy spinning inward towards my spleen, liver and adrenals. My reproductive center became warm, like the steaming cauldron I had seen in Dreaming, and the force of my will forged, as though the fibers of my intent emerging from my umbilical region were being woven into a thick, sturdy rope.

"That is a very powerful and energizing breath!" I exclaimed after having completed his instructions. "My vision is enhanced. I feel revitalized."

"There are many things that can be done with it," don Juan added. "For example, a healer can send the energy into his hands, to sensitize them for a body scan, as Chon does. The breath can be used to maintain vitality and well-being. It can also be enhanced by allowing a further opening of the head, hands and feet, when pulling in energy from external sources, such as trees, the Earth, the sky or the sun. All of our tired, sick energy can be released on the liquid out breath, as the energy moves down the front of the body. This can be done by embracing the trunk of a tree and releasing on the exhale, pushing the abdomen in, or by allowing the exhaled energy to drain through the feet into the Earth, or by doing the in-breath lying on one's back on a stone facing up at the sun, and then executing the out-breath rolled over with the abdomen on the boulder, releasing the tired or diseased energy from the center of will, through the stone and into the Earth. Any tired or ill energy can always be released on that out-breath which travels down the front, by pushing the abdomen in while exhaling.

"This breath also enhances the sexual organs and feeds them with a fresh supply of warm and vitalized energy, which may be stored there in order to cultivate potency, creativity, health and longevity. For a shaman or a healer, sexual energy is very important, as we have discussed. Remember though, that sexual energy is often utilized differently by shamans, healers, and sorcerers than it is by ordinary people. Shamans and healers need a large dose of sexual energy to do their work and so this breath is invaluable. I would say, however, that it is also extremely beneficial for the ordinary man or woman, so that they may maintain or cultivate well-being and heightened energy in a relationship."

"I'm glad to hear that these practices are also helpful for people who are not actively becoming shamans, sorcerers, or healers," I reflected gratefully.

"Everything we have shared with you since your first arrival at my home over one week ago is of the utmost benefit," don Juan confirmed.

"How often should the fire breath be done, don Juan?"

"Just as Dreaming should be done every night to enhance well-being and power, so should the fire breath be done at least once a day, preferably when one is relaxing in the fresh air, as we are now."

"Are there other shamanic methods that raise the sexual energy besides Dreaming snake and fire breath?" I asked.

"Yes. There are several. A shaman may use rattling with a very special kind of rattle, which can reproduce a sound similar to the shaking of a rattlesnake's tail when it gives warning before it rears to strike. This is the reason rattles have been employed since the beginning of time. They evoke a snake's trance state and the shaman is able to ride the sound and intensify it to reach the desired heights. Another method is the singing of special snake songs that are given in Dreaming for that express purpose. Healers and shamans often sing these songs to raise the energy while they work. When they sing a song given in Dreaming, they are bridging the power and in a sense are Dreaming awake. Yet another method is to dance, but in order to raise the sexual energy up the spine through dancing, the spine must be kept very supple. There are magnificent snake dancers among the different desert tribes. However, many people lose the flexibility necessary to dance snake through repetitive movements, thoughts, and behaviors that stiffen the body. Fluidity is the key."

"Are there ways to regain the flexibility?" I asked him.

"The most important movement for the back is to stretch and crack the spine often. This releases tension and penned-up energy we are holding. Then one may seek to slow and extend the stretch. For the snake, movements should be graceful, undulating and powerful, never jerky and overly explosive. That is a waste of energy. The movement should start in the lower spine, in the areas where sexual arousal first occurs, and should then follow the flow upward in a rippling motion until the energy fountains above the head like a flame. The arms then float softly upward, extending their length like the flame shifting in a soft breeze. The arms are then stretched out sideways in flight, as snake becomes eagle, still keeping the spine supple and rippling.

"Dances such as these, special power sounds and songs will definitely raise the sexual energy. The healer or shaman's force will then be maximized for the work they intend to do. The special rattles, individual sounds, songs, and the particular qualities of the dance are all found in Dreaming first and then bridged into curing ceremonies, healings, or shamanic work. Always proceed in a sacred way, remembering that this energy is among the most potent in creation. Ask permission. It is a very ancient energy and has its own wisdom. You do not want to anger, disgust, or defile it under any circumstances, especially not once it has been awakened.

"My feeling is that most people today prefer to remain in slumber. It is easier to be sloppy. Once the serpent has been awakened there is no excuse, and if you make a snake angry it will strike. The careless individual still gets bitten when he or she is clumsy. Ignorance is no defense. The difference is that the careless person does not know where the bite came from.

"Shamans take many precautions so that they might raise and awaken the energy in the best possible circumstances, into an energetic space that it will not find completely distasteful. Once the energy is above a certain level, once it becomes celestial, it becomes very selective."

"Is there anything else I should know, don Juan?"

"You did very well Dreaming snake. That taught you a great deal, but as I told you the serpent can move even higher. Don't try to hold it. Beyond fountaining out the top of the head, it can actually fly, but only when the practitioner is ready and that takes a long time, perhaps a lifetime. You should know that bringing the energy back down to its nest in the base of the spine and the sexual organs is as important as raising it up, or awakening it. When the energy returns, it should not crash but rather descend gracefully and filled with vitality, never depleted. This is of great importance. Hence the fire breath, as Chon calls it. This is the way to return the energy replenished. It must melt down the front, never fall down the back, understand?"

"Yes, thank you. I see. You've told me so many things that people don't know about working with sexual energy, don Juan. This is knowledge people need to have. Not only do many lack understanding of what to do with or how properly to honor their sexual energies, there are those who try to raise this energy—which some disciplines have called kundalini—carelessly."

"That is madness," don Juan stated firmly. "Let's take a walk around. What do you say?" he suggested, slapping his thighs, standing and stretching his spine.

"Absolutely," I replied.

We ambled along pleasurably to the other side of the park where a group of musicians were setting up to play their first tune. Their four-piece ensemble consisted of a folk harpist, an accordion player, a guitarist, and a base guitarist. All of them appeared to be in their fifties and had the robust look of happy, well-fed Mexicans. While we waited, we mingled with the passersby who were collecting to enjoy the music and who would occasionally put a few pesos into the group's instrument cases. The concert began in quite a lively way, consisting of rancheras, which have a frisky two-step dance beat, and Veracruzanas, which play the joyous central melody on the folk harp.

I felt the bouncy rhythm and had a desire to shuffle my feet, which I did discreetly so as not to attract undue attention to myself. Soon scores of locals were strolling the park—women with small children, students on lunch break, ice cream and balloon vendors, businesspeople, literally every type of citizen from that area, including little old ladies, out from the woodworks with their granddaughters to help them. It turned into quite a festive affair. The musicians played for about an hour and then finally broke up for lunch. The crowd dispersed and everyone made their way back home or to restaurants for the midday meal. Don Juan suggested that we do the same and we walked across the street and around the corner to Hong Li's.

A colorfully painted, open-mouthed dragon awaited us at the entrance to the restaurant. I gave don Juan a conspirator's glance as we were ushered into the dimly lit, tastefully furnished dining room by a delicate young woman who spoke Spanish, but with a distinct Chinese accent. After seating us at a well-chosen, private table, she went back into the kitchen and, shortly afterwards, Hong Li came out to introduce himself.

In broken Spanish he profusely welcomed us, insisting that we accept our lunch without charge and allow him to select for us from the best he had to offer that day. We graciously accepted and thanked him and he scurried off into the kitchen, shouting rapidly in Chinese. "That fellow is one of Celestina's clients," don Juan reminded me. "She never ceases to amaze me."

It was a pleasure to see don Juan and doña Celestina being treated with such respect by someone outside of the Native and shamanic circles. Hong Li's tone was that reserved for addressing a venerable old wise one, something highly valued

in his culture, and this came across, even through the somewhat choppy linguistic barrier.

Hong Li himself was a small, slight Chinese man, perhaps
in his late sixties, who evidently was experiencing good for-
tune in his business venture. Chinese food has become quite
popular in Mexico, as it has almost everywhere in the world,
and many Chinese emigrate to open restaurants there. The
recipes and ingredients used are at times more authentic than
fare served across the border in the United States, due to more
lenient import and export regulations.

We were brought a large china pot of chrysanthemum tea
and a bowl of unrefined rock sugar crystals. Shortly following,
two large bowls of thick rice soup accented with pieces of
aged, preserved duck egg, what the Chinese call "2,000-year-
old egg," arrived. Upon finishing the soup we were treated to
an appetizer called "crystal prawns," gigantic blue prawns
which may be obtained only from the Gulf of Cortez, perhaps
150 kilometers to the south. Although cleaned and cooked,
they had been prepared in a manner that enhanced the natural
translucence of their uncooked state, and were served in a nest
of colorful shredded cucumber, carrot, and crisped transparent
bean thread noodle.

Don Juan seemed truly impressed with the ceremonial
and artistic attention given to honor the food's preparation
and presentation, and with the quality and flavor of the food.
He asked me curiously if the Chinese also honor the spirit of
the creatures they receive as food. I told him that I did not
know for sure, but that I was certain that they honored their
tea, and that they appeared to have a very good rapport with
plants, judging by their herbal medicine.

After having an appropriate length of time to relax and sip
our tea, two portions of green-tea-smoked and pressed duck
arrived. Following the beautiful meal, Hong Li returned to ask
us if we had enjoyed it, and brought out his mother to meet

don Juan. She was an exquisite Chinese woman in perhaps her mid-eighties, who spoke no Spanish at all. When we rose to leave, after all the thanks and introductions, Hong Li spoke to me.

"Thank you for bringing your elder to meet my elder," he said in his best Spanish.

"Thank you in return," I said and bowed slightly.

After we had walked out the door and were on our way back to the jeep, don Juan spoke of his impressions of the experience. "They know of the value of energy and longevity," he said. "That is good."

I agreed, and we got into the jeep to drive back to the house.

PRACTICE NINE

A SIMPLE VERSION OF FIRE BREATH

1. Stand with your feet shoulder width apart, legs relaxed yet rooted, knees slightly bent. Hang your arms at your sides, loose and limp, fingers slightly curled. Be sure your spine is straight and your neck and shoulders are relaxed, maintaining good posture. Gaze softly into the distance.

2. Now breathe in through the nostrils, pulling up on the muscles of the perineum and contracting the abdomen on the inhale. The energy should rise in the form of heat, to the area of contraction, which in this case is the umbilical area. Continue to breathe in this way until you feel the heat.

3. Next, attempt to pull the warm energy up your spine and into the area of your back heart. This is done by straightening the small of the back on the inhale, which is still accompanied by an abdominal contraction, with a softer perineal pull. As the energy rises to the back of your solar plexus, it will become even warmer. Now, with additional inhales, accompanied by abdominal contractions, open the back shoulder blades by flexing them, curving your shoulders slightly inward. This will raise the energy into the back heart area and you will feel heat expanding into your arms and hands, which may throb or perspire. You may also feel flushed. This is normal.

4. Straighten the curve at the back of the neck on the next inhale. An abdominal contraction is required, but the perineal pull is no longer necessary. Try to inhale with the back of your throat and ears—your gills, if you will—for you are now breathing more energy than air.

5. One snort through the back sinuses, accompanied by an abdominal contraction, will send the breath into your inner eye, which will heat up, thereby expanding.

   This "eye" is located about one inch back into the forehead, directly centered above the nose between the brows, perhaps three-quarters of an inch above them. The eye may throb and open if you are ready. This is essential for Seeing certain kinds of energy during a healing. Tip your head slightly forward and allow the heat to become moist as it moves toward the front, the liquid side of your body. You may feel an actual drip, as if warm oil or honey is oozing one drop at a time through your forehead.

6. Now straighten your head and the drip will accumulate on your soft palate. Swallow this life-giving elixir and it will spread into your throat, opening this center and melting downward.

7. The inhale for the front of the body is now a soft inhale accompanied by a deep abdominal expansion. This allows the energy to fill the front, as though you were pouring it into a wine skin.

8. Inhale the warm liquid energy into the heart area by expanding the upper lungs. This will stimulate soft, gentle feelings of love. As the energy melts down further, it will hit the solar plexus and spin to the sides. Massage the warm current into your internal organs, the spleen to the left and the liver, pancreas and gall bladder to the right. Remember to continue expanding your abdomen on the inhale.

9. From there, the energy proceeds downward diagonally from each side to collect in your reproductive area. An in-breath with an abdominal expansion will fill the bottom of your energetic lake.

10. Finally, a gentle abdominal contraction on the exhale will return the energy to be stored in the center of will, behind the navel.

SISTERHOOD
AND
BROTHERHOOD

AFTER EACH DAY'S TRAINING SESSION, I WAS always allowed some time to myself to write, to process, or to practice what I had learned on my own, if this was appropriate. I spent many hours writing at the old medical desk in my room, or taking walks alone in the desert. In the case of the fire breath, I found that it was quite a portable task and very easy and enjoyable to practice almost anywhere at any time. I even tried it lying down and found that the out-breath was most conducive to restful, deep, Dreaming sleep. The in-breath, on the other hand, was very energizing in the morning, and especially compatible with an early morning walk, or a warm outdoor shower and a cup of ephedra tea, which was available almost every morning in the kitchen.

I enjoyed my solitary time, but even more than that I relished the heightened energy we experienced being together in the same locale, all of us under one roof for a while. Chon addressed these issues in his next lesson. We were cleaning plants at the dining table under the portico of the patio in the late afternoon.

"I want to talk with you about trust," Chon began, as we separated the leaves from a large toloache plant. "I know that you trust us all implicitly, and that is good, for it is a very important issue in this work and one that is often violated. Many apprentices do not get their initiations into the sexual energies through ritual, ceremony, and practices as we are doing with you. Rather, at some point, they may find themselves being manipulated by their mentor and learn about misuses of the energy when they claw their way out of the situation."

I looked at him with raised eyebrows as I put some prickly seed pods to one side.

"There are various types of manipulation that I want to tell you about, so that you will be able to recognize them and help potential clients if you ever choose to do this work. One common form entails a leap in Dreaming. The sorcerer will go with his or her Dream body to the apprentice while the apprentice is asleep, and engage them in a form of energetic intercourse that binds the apprentice's sexual energies and will into the service of the sorcerer. These are possession techniques, not unlike the ones doña Celestina has been teaching you.

"Some sorcerers will also attempt to have unsolicited sexual relations with their apprentices. The technique is one of building the power of the sorcerer up, while wearing the apprentice down. The more I can convince you that I am the powerful one, the more of your energy you will transfer to me, hoping that I will recognize you and transfer power back to you. The sorcerer who manipulates in this way naturally looks very charismatic to the apprentices whose energy he or she is wearing. After all, the sorcerer is strutting around in their own energy. Naturally the apprentices, or would-be apprentices, find him or her desirable."

"I've heard of this kind of situation among gurus and their devotees and among charismatic preachers and their flock," I commented. It then took me quite a while to explain the concept of gurus and preachers to Chon. He listened with keen interest and amusement. Afterwards I asked him, "Why do you think people fall for these tricks?"

"Perhaps it has something to do with their egos," he suggested, "and wanting to feel self-important. Perhaps it is exactly the opposite, they feel worthless. Or perhaps they simply have never been told that this is an inappropriate practice between teacher and apprentice."

"I must admit that I have never heard a sorcerer discuss this etiquette before," I agreed.

"Exactly my point, for who would discuss it if they intend to break it?" Chon replied. "Some sorcerers even elicit a slave-and-master relationship from their apprentices and this is another abuse. A task master is very different from an oppressor. If you ever take clients the way doña Celestina and I do, and you listen to their plights, you will come to recognize these situations. You will also See them when you scan the person energetically. Knowing the nature of the beast is the first step to disassembling its power."

"Yes, I can see that. Otherwise I too might be mystified. But I have never heard of these things being spoken of out in the open," I urged him.

"That is why they are called occult practices, Merlina."

"How can people be sure of what they are getting themselves into, then?" I challenged.

"That's a very good question." Chon paused to reflect. "The first safeguards, that are barely present in this modern world, were the sisterhoods and brotherhoods."

"Do you mean nuns and monks, priests and priestesses, or fraternal orders?" I asked, and explained the differences between each to Chon as he again listened, rapt with interest.

"We have seen Christian nuns and monks, and also priests among the Maya for centuries. Recently, Buddhist monks and nuns have been journeying to the temple sites, but I did not know of the concept of priestesses in your culture or of these fraternal orders. I would say that when they are behaving according to their ideals, they are not dissimilar to what I am talking about, but the Maya have seen many Christian priests behaving badly throughout their history in the Americas.

"What I am speaking of is not quite the same. One difference is the age of admission, for example. The old way was to have female children learn from the council of women shaman-priestesses, and the male children would learn from the warriors and shaman-priests. Children would spend all of their time with a same-sex elder, older same-sex siblings and the shamans, healers, priests, warriors, artisans, and so forth of their same sex. During this period they would be given all the necessary lessons to assure their survival and start them on the path to wisdom in an environment that was non-threatening, sexually speaking. There they could learn about sexual energy and power in a situation that was not sexually combative or exploitative. This is something that seems to be sorely lacking in your culture now, and through contact with the modern world, indigenous peoples are having to fight to keep it from vanishing within our own. It is such a shame to send a young person out into the world without protection or the knowledge to discern what's what!"

"I couldn't agree with you more, Chon." I said. "This is something we should try to rebuild into our lives if we want to improve our society."

"Perhaps it will happen," he said hopefully. "Once children reached adolescence, they underwent a puberty initiation by their same-sex shamans, among fellow same-sex initiates. Even after the initiation, they always had contact with their circle of elders, and of course with their peers. They might even grow to be shamans, healer-priests, or warriors themselves someday, but even if they did not, they took part in the council circle in order to receive shared knowledge and to continue learning.

"Problems seem to arise when knowledge is withheld or concealed for the wrong purpose, and so it was beneficial in adulthood to apprentice from a shaman, healer, or sorcerer, so that the veil might be lifted from the eyes."

"Why is knowledge concealed, Chon?" I asked. This was a question I had been burning to voice for years.

"There are several reasons why knowledge and energy mask themselves. One is for privacy, which is quite understandable. One is for protection. Sometimes one must conceal one's ability to do good, for example, or one will draw attack or be flooded by the impatient. Conversely, sorcerers may at times conceal in order to deceive and do harm. That is why Seeing energy is so important, Merlina. Energy may conceal itself, or mask itself, but it doesn't lie. Energy carries within it the code of its function. If you can read the signs, they are as plain as day. This is something a H'men must learn to do, to read the signs clearly and to interpret Dreams accurately. It takes many years of practice and study even if you have the gift, which you do.

"In apprenticing oneself to a sorcerer, healer-priest, or shaman, the apprentice may cross over to work with an opposite-sex mentor. A certain level of maturity is required for this and yes, there is an 'appropriate etiquette,' as you put it. The proper way is for a feeling of sisterhood and brotherhood to be established, so that no one would ever dream of violating that sacred space. Naturally romantic love, and deeper spiritual love, does occasionally occur; the practitioners are expected to work out the details in a mature and energetically clean way. If they are going to continue in the work, this is necessary. Some practitioners marry. This is fine. Some experience a form of energetic union that extends beyond the boundaries of the bodies we now occupy."

"You always have a way of making everything so ultimately beautiful, Chon," I exclaimed.

"That is the way I see it. I truly prefer these types of relationships to the undercut garden variety so rampant in the world now. It's not people's fault, really. There is knowledge which, for one reason or another, they have not been exposed to and that is tragic, for in most instances it is a case of manipulation, control, or oppression."

"I've got to get you into politics!" I teased.

"No thanks, I can do my best work sharing what I have to offer right here."

"Do practitioners ever live in communal homes, like nuns and monks live in monasteries?" I asked.

"I suppose that would be an option, but it is really not the point. The point is to get out into the world and do the work. Many native peoples had communal dwellings, however these were extended family dwellings for the most part, or ceremonial meeting places. They still exist today to some degree. But if I understand you correctly, you are referring to communal dwellings especially designed to further the individual energetic or spiritual practice of the residents, while allowing them to be in like company, no?"

"Right." I nodded.

"Well, that can be established by an individual practitioner if they so desire. Look at Celestina here. She is a perfect example of the way in which it is done. She has become powerful enough to support herself with her work and has acquired quite a reputation. She is able to attract apprentices and has devised a household that allows them to live with her, while learning to support themselves by earning their keep and enhancing the power here. If they stay with her long enough, they learn everything they need, based on Celestina's Seeing, and they do not want for anything, although she works their backsides off. And you notice that they are all of the same sex, and exactly the right age to begin, considering the harsh circumstances they came from. No Indian's life is ever easy, and as I told you before, in an ideal environment they would begin to learn even earlier."

"Do you mean that doña Celestina will train some of them to be witches?" I asked, astonished.

"Of course," Chon laughed and wiped his big grin with his hand. "What do you think this is? She's teaching you, isn't she?"

"But I thought . . ."

"Haven't you noticed that there are times when none of them can be found about, and that she speaks with them privately much more than explaining mere household chores, even considering her perfectionist standards, would require?"

"Yes, but they're so young!"

"That's the way it is. If Celestina doesn't catch them now, they'll become fodder for a string of mistakes and won't have another chance until they hit an even more desperate do-or-die crisis later on in life. I tell you Celestina is a marvel. She even keeps a few extra rooms for cohorts of her own generation!"

Now I had to smile. Chon was absolutely right.

"When you came to see me in the jungle, I was staying with a fellow practitioner who does basically the same thing. Don't you remember Esmeralda?" Esmeralda is a delightful Native woman whom I often see on my frequent visits to southern Mexico. She travels among various indigenous communities and supports herself by being perhaps the only woman within a community who will prepare and offer food for sale. To say that she is an excellent and creative cook of traditional and regional foods is an understatement. "Running a little open-air restaurant wherever she happens to be is Esmeralda's way of supporting herself and finding young girls who want to work, so that she can teach them. Oh, by the way, she asked me to tell you hello!" Chon said.

"Please give her my best regards and a warm hug when you see her again," I replied sincerely. "How is she?"

"Just fine. You'll have to come down to our part of Mexico again sometime soon and see for yourself. Now do you remember those boys that used to come to her house, the ones she told you were her sons?"

"I never believed that," I replied. "Nor did I believe that she was your sister. There is no resemblance between any of you. Now I know what all of you meant, though. You are family in spirit and practice."

"That's right! Just as you are our little deer. The sorcerer's code of ethics! Eh?" We both had to laugh. "Well, I was going to tell you that those boys were apprentices to us both, but I guess you've already figured that out."

"You even told me once, Chon, but at that point I didn't know what to believe, as I'm sure you can understand."

"We don't mean to be so tricky," he pleaded. "We are telling the truth. It's just that we're being discreet."

"Do you think that it's possible for people from my culture to learn to respect one another in these ways?" I pondered.

"I certainly hope so. As you have told me, your culture already has many similar structures in place, such as these monasteries and fraternal meeting houses. The problem seems to be that these societies and orders, as you call them, though they are same-sex, provide no instruction in the best possible expressions of sexual energy beyond celibacy or perhaps marriage. There seem to be no energetic teachings. This repression, combined with a lack of knowledge, causes people to act out in the most atrocious ways."

"It's not just our culture, either, and I think that the world is getting into trouble because of it. I have a theory that this is why shamans and healers are now willing to share some of their traditional knowledge."

"Good idea." Chon replied and we cleared off the table.

PRACTICE TEN

SHAMANIC CIRCLES

1. Form a circle of women and girls of all ages where knowledge is shared openly with wisdom and without taboos. These circles can be formed around a theme such as herbal medicine, midwifery, sacred ceremony, ritual art, or even the preparation of special foods. It is essential that the wisdom of all present be honored, that no themes be unacceptable for discussion or sacred work, and that a level of trust, respect, appreciation, and lasting friendship be fostered.

2. A circle of males and boys of all ages would be based upon the same values, the wisdom of all the cycles of life. Here same-sex knowledge may be shared openly without fear. Themes might include survival skills, vision quests and sweat lodges, useful trades, gardening, or herbal medicine.

3. The important point is for the knowledge of experience to be shared and passed on. Chon feels such circles create a safe haven, a place to experiment and learn regardless of age, a place to seek counsel. They are the forerunner of shamanic sisterhoods and brotherhoods, mentors and wise men and women, a concept all but lost in our society and desperately needed.

DREAMING
THE BODY

THE FOLLOWING MORNING CHON SUGGESTED THAT we drive to the *hierbería* (shop that sells medicinal herbs), El Tecolote, which was not terribly far from doña Celestina's home on the outskirts of San Luis.

"I hope that you're not getting tired of me," he said jokingly as we approached the jeep, gently putting his hand on my shoulder.

"What, are you kidding?" I looked at his beaming smile. "This is wonderful! It's such a pleasure to see you up here in the desert, so close to the U.S. border. It feels very different from going to see you in the jungles and highlands."

"That's good, because we have more work to do before I can turn you over again to one of my esteemed associates," he said with a wink.

I could tell by Chon's levity that he was in a cheerful mood, but honestly I had not ever seen him otherwise. Although he's never frivolous, he always seems lighthearted, even when he's extremely concerned. I'm sure this is one reason he's so popular with his patients. I unlocked the door and we loaded some sacks into the back seat.

"So, what's on the agenda for today?" I asked as we got into the jeep.

"Well, first we go to El Tecolote, otherwise I sense I'll never get there!" he laughed. "Then, I'd like to talk with you about the double."

The double, or *el doble* as it is called in Spanish among Native peoples from Mexico to South America, is the consummate shamanic art, which enables shamans, healers, and sorcerers to perform many seemingly miraculous energetic feats. Everything from bilocation to shapeshifting, to possessions, journeying into other realms of energy, or bringing back energetic gifts and powers, is accomplished through the double, which is neither a visualization nor a projection, but rather a fully-honed energy body blazing with life force.

The development of the double is the attainment that every practitioner works toward, and it can take decades for some to accomplish. I was thrilled that this would be the topic of our lesson, since there is never too much that one can learn about it.

When we arrived at the hierbería, I parked in the back lot. Hierbería El Tecolote, "The Owl" in English, has gained a reputation throughout Mexico for being one of the most comprehensive herbal vendors in the country. The store itself is unassuming, medium-sized, and always kept very dark. The shelves on every wall are lined with bottles and jars of roots, leaves, stems, seeds, flowers, nuts, thorns, tubers, bulbs, fungi, every conceivable part of what grows from the earth. Rare, hard-to-find plants may be obtained and the specialty is combinations, potions, and the like, for most of the known maladies and many that I have never even heard of.

We entered the shop, which did not have any customers at the moment. A short, somber, dark-skinned man with wavy black hair was behind the counter, dusting the jars with a feather duster. I knew that he could not be the owner, for he is a much older man and a long-time acquaintance of Chon's. I browsed the shelves while Chon talked with the man and told him what he was looking for. Evidently, the attendant was one of the owner's sons.

While I waited for Chon to make his purchases and trades, he confided to me that among his favorite mixtures are those for gout and high blood sugar, which are very effective and contain plants that he cannot find in the Maya region. He also informed me that El Tecolote offers many excellent remedies for women's complaints, reproductive tract tumors, too much or too little fertility, and formulations for men to treat prostate problems, impotence, and the like. Then he giggled. "I don't need any of those myself. The important point is that there are plants that can help someone who is ill to recover their sexual energy, which is crucial to replenish if the patient is going to heal and be vital."

"Do illnesses deplete sexual energy Chon?" I asked him quietly. Several old women had entered and waited behind us at the counter.

"Some do," he whispered. "But usually it is the other way around. If your sexual energy is depleted, you'll get sick. We'll talk more outside." He glanced at the women and whispered to the owner's son that he should send one of the older women, who was standing supported by another's arm, around for a treatment. The older woman was quite decrepit, although she did not appear to be ill.

"Yes, I will," the attendant said, nodding, as he passed multiple bundles wrapped in an off-white paper across the counter to Chon. "You should come by and visit with my father later in the week if you can," he said. "He'll be glad to see you. Today he is with his sister. Come by in the late afternoon, after he takes his nap, if you like."

"I will," Chon said. "Give him my regards when he returns."

We put all of the bundles into Chon's sacks and walked out to the jeep. I was burning with questions, and Chon suggested that we put the sacks into the back and take a stroll. We ended up in a neighborhood park and sat down under a shady palo verde tree.

"What's the connection between depleted sexual energy and illness?" I asked him finally.

He smiled, knowing how long I had been holding that question. "Sexual energy is one of the batteries of the double, and it is the double that has the body's energetic blueprint. It transmits knowledge as energy to the physical body and drives it in the same way that you drive your jeep. Leaking or losing this energy makes the vehicle not function at top speed. Also miscommunications can occur, sort of like two people trying to talk on the phone without enough line in between them. Or, like the machines that make tortillas, the energy body will make a quantity of whatever is needed and will make it properly, but if you need twenty and pull the plug at ten, well, all you're going to get are ten."

"So sexual energy is intimately connected to the double," I surmised. "It is an essential component."

"Yes, Merlina. That's the lesson for today. Sexual energy is creative and so it is a foundation energy for Dreaming. The process begins, as you know, with the task of Dreaming the body. Each night during sleep, the energy body goes through stages. The first stage is bodily repairs. The energy body spends at least several hours per night inside the bones, blood, organs, and skin, renewing the physical body. It will spend more time if the body is ill. Part of the fuel for this process is our own sexual energy, so if the individual needs to heal, herbs that are tonic and fortify the sexual energies should be used in conjunction with the other remedies. Otherwise, the energy body may spend all the available energy trying to make repairs, and it may not even have enough, leaving the body in a state of fatigue and malaise.

"Following the healing sleep, the energy body has the opportunity to replenish itself with sources of external energy, available to it by virtue of its nature as energy, but which must be predigested, if you will, by the energy body in order to make them utilizable to the physical body. For this purpose the energy body leaves the physical body in order to swim in the realms of external energy. Unskilled Dreamers are amorphous blobs when they leave the body. They absorb little energy. They are often timid and can't stay out of the physical body long without running out of steam and having to return. They have no stamina, and stamina is the rule. It's a rule of survival. When you run out of the energy to Dream, the energy body is pulled back into the physical body.

"Not only do practitioners seek to extend their energy absorption-time by becoming more efficient and adaptable to higher and higher grades of free energy, they also seek to hone fully the Dream body while out of the physical body during these extended explorations. This is begun by Dreaming every facet of the physical body as it lies sleeping in the actual location and position in which it can be found. The Dreamer is the energy body. The Dreamer seeks to Dream a full-fledged body of higher energy that gazes at and then is able to walk away from the sleeping physical body. There should be no timid attachment whatsoever, no umbilical cord, nothing. The only energy left with the physical body should be that which is required to maintain a slow heartbeat and soft, slow respiration.

"All forms of energy taken in by the Dreaming double should then be concentrated within it during Dreaming and bridged into the physical body upon awakening. This energy may then be circulated and the physical body will step up, to operate more and more upon free energy, not using up its vital reserves. There are important reasons for this that Juan and I will discuss with you later.

"Your case was easy, Merlina. I truly believe, as I Saw the day we first met in Dreaming and in Mexico, that you were born with a developed energy body. That is very rare. I, in all my journeys, have never seen that among human beings before, and you are human. I don't know what it means, but that is the reason I was moved to work with you. Normally I never would have been interested in doing this kind of energetic work with someone from outside my culture. For you, the task was to realize what you had, so that you could put it into action in a more sophisticated way, for there are many places one may go with a developed energy body. Your energy body has true genius. I haven't found a way to improve on its artistry, besides showing it things that it has not seen before, possibilities that it has not yet been exposed to, and of course, by showing it how to become more 'fuel efficient,' to use an American term, and access more energy in myriad ways."

"Everything you have taught me, Chon, has been fine art, and has expanded my growth in inconceivable ways. I am eternally grateful," I said lovingly and respectfully.

"What puzzles me," I added, "is how, after struggling to attain the Dream body, one could devalue all that hard work by misusing the possibilities. Although you showed me over and over that my Dream body was already out and about, and acting on its own, you're right—I had to be convinced, not because I didn't believe you, but because I felt I needed that touchstone. It took me seventeen years to Dream the body, completing the task as you describe it."

"Perhaps you did need to see it, although you know I certainly wouldn't fib to you," Chon gave a sly grin. "That length of time to ascertain what you already had in motion, could still be considered short by some, who strive for even longer just to forge their energy body. You ask how after such a struggle they could desire to misuse it? That is the bent of one's character, Merlina. Some people don't learn of healing or artistry when they pursue this path. They are looking for the big payoff, but are coarse and don't recognize quality when it presents itself. Concentrated quality is the key, not vulgar quantity. Like a fine perfume, concentrated quality will not go sour and it will yield much more in the long run.

"So yes, there are many who use their doubles for sexual exploitation and other antics we discussed yesterday. They miss the point and when it comes to final acts before leaving this world, they are tethered by their attachments and haven't got the capacity even to conceive of what to do next or where to go. It doesn't end well."

"Both you and don Juan keep speaking to me of final things. I feel as though you are preparing me," I said.

"We are," Chon said with a serious tone. "We have much more to share with you before we'll consider letting you get away from us this time." He gave me a sinister smirk. "I think perhaps, not to change the subject of course, but I think your energy body would help you in teaching Dreaming, the way mine helps me."

I felt an energetic jolt. There was something about the way he said "the way mine helps me," as if he were speaking of now. Simply being with Chon can become non-ordinary. He has an astounding capability to bring his double into the waking world as an identical replica of his physical body, and one can never really be sure with which one is dealing. This was my situation.

I have seen him completely shift people who come to his herb stand when he is doubled. Even though they are locals, they'll walk away and forget what else they were doing, or whatever else they needed, and wander—sometimes even getting lost for brief periods in their own home territory.

On many occasions I have been with him only to find that a scene or experience in the waking world will suddenly turn phantasmagorical. I'll realize, astounded at that moment, that I am actually with his double. In order to protect myself from being caught unawares, I've developed a method of buffering myself, which is simply to assume that I'm always dealing with his double, and therefore always Dreaming awake. This is the only way that I can keep him from catching me off balance.

He seems to prefer that I remain in this state of hyperalertness, and will occasionally test me. The confounding thing about the whole process is that, once started, it is hard to stop. Don Juan and doña Celestina also started pushing me there, and I found that it became very difficult to find moments when I could be certain I wasn't Dreaming. To keep from going crazy, I simply decided that I was always Dreaming—a moment of decision which, when it came, Chon rejoiced in.

That was when they told me that this is the first step of bringing the double into the waking physical world, as they do. The double becomes indistinguishable from the physical body, and yet it has access to its powers in Dreaming. It operates fully in the waking world, and one becomes one's double. A transformation occurs, because where the other self (the non-Dreaming self) goes is beyond me. Chon says that once one truly Dreams with the whole being, there is no non-Dreaming self. It disappears. It simply falls off like a cheap suit.

I took a deep breath. Again, somehow, Chon had led me into a very peculiar energetic state. I felt as if some unknown, or perhaps supremely known but not acknowledged, force were just about to be revealed.

"We'll get there," Chon said and touched my hand to steady me. "There are Dreaming practices that one may use within the body to help heal it. One may Dream inside a diseased area of the body and clean it out. It is also possible to pull energy into desired areas of the physical body during Dreaming. One may begin these methods before developing the double, but once it has been developed, their power and effectiveness are magnified.

"As you know, I employ a tremendous amount of Dreaming energy in my work as a healer. Tomorrow I intend to show you some more of what I do. I'll set up a consultation area in one of doña Celestina's back rooms and we'll work on clients together."

I was very excited by the possibility. "How will people know that you are here in the area, Chon?"

In the Mayan jungles and highlands, it was always by word of mouth that people knew of Chon, since he traveled around so much. People would literally line up in the early hours of the morning if word was given as to when and where he would be. Often there would be a line into the late afternoon.

"Doña Celestina and don Juan have been letting people know, and I've paid a few visits in the area while you were working with them. It won't be like it is at home. I've asked my acquaintances to be discreet, so that we won't be overwhelmed with people. I want you to really have the opportunity to experience what the energy body can do in a healing session."

That thought kept me captivated. The light was now changing and so we decided to start walking back to the jeep. Chon had calmed my fears and piqued my interest all in one graceful stroke. I looked forward to working with him and knew that it would be a day I'd never forget.

PRACTICE ELEVEN

DREAMING THE BODY

1. The goal of this practice is the full honing and development of a Dreaming double, a fully articulated energy body with the ability to operate as a physical body on a higher level, a body that is capable of maintaining the life force on its own at the moment of transformations at death.

2. This process is a continual one. The practitioner is constantly seeking refinements, even as the moment of death occurs and beyond. This is accomplished by applying the artistry of the double to every endeavor—but first, of course, one must strive to develop it.

3. The process is always initiated with the same Dreaming task. First strive to Dream that you are in your body, filled with well-being and that you are gazing upon your own sleeping physical body as it lies in the position and place where you genuinely are.

4. There should be no silver cord of any kind. This is not an astral projection, which only removes a small portion of energy and awareness from the physical body and tethers this with a cord from the umbilicus, beyond the length of which one may not travel. Doubling removes every portion of energy that is not required to maintain a slow heartbeat and respiration, and affords the opportunity to express that energy in this realm, as well as in others.

5. Gaze at your sleeping body, and verify for your satisfaction that it is truly yourself in the proper place and time. You needn't worry that your physical body will open its eyes and die of fright upon seeing you looking back at it. You are already in that position. Your body will remain motionless, but alive.

6. Explore the feeling of being in your energy body. Do not attempt to go too far on the first try. Rather, concentrate on being fully present and taking in your surroundings. Protect your body first with your Dreaming intent, and then perhaps take a short stroll.

7. As with shapeshifting, there is no need to return to your sleeping body. When your energy is used up you will return to it automatically and gently. The more energy you build for the work, the more time you will be able to double. Some practitioners, like Chon, can remained doubled indefinitely, can wake up into their double and can actually go about their daily affairs exclusively with their Dreaming double!

ENERGY
HEALING

A MIST OF AROMATIC COPAL SMOKE BLENDED WITH THE freshness of pale early morning light. Chon was in the back area of doña Celestina's home, singing to himself as cheerfully as a bird while he swept out the vacant room in the separate section behind the patio. The four girls were helping him move a long, narrow, sturdy wooden table through the doorway, following his instructions. It was placed centrally and then covered with a folded straw mat that would allow it to serve as the examination and massage table.

I greeted everyone and walked into the room. Even though the space was almost bare—just the long table placed in the center, a few straight-backed wooden chairs against the walls, several sacks of plants near the door, and a small, square wooden table with one drawer positioned in one of the back corners—I felt Chon's unmistakable presence permeating every inch of it.

"Have you had your breakfast?" he asked with a smile as bright as the new light.

I nodded.

"Good. So have I. Let's get to work. Why don't you sit down in that chair over there and we'll go over some of the basics?"

I pulled up a chair and sat directly across from him in the rays of morning sunshine that streamed through the open doorway.

"First, I want you to breathe as Juan showed you the other day. Do one complete circle from the base of the spine, up the back and then down the front returning to the center of will. This cleanses your energy field. Now, let's add some copal."

Chon got up to retrieve the censor. He then fanned the smoke at me with his hands and even blew it at me with a gentle all-over sweeping breath.

"Copal smoke has a feminine spirit," he said as he worked, "unlike tobacco, which is masculine. The essence is cleansing, penetrating, and protective, yet neutral and non-intrusive, perfect for healers. Now close your eyes. You can gaze at your client through the smoke by softening your focus a bit and allowing the haze to wash the eyes and the vision. Riding the smoke with the eyes will strip what is behind it of illusory coverings. It will allow you to see the energy in various centers and in the organs, as well a give you a view of the skeleton, and the energetic entity that is navigating this form. Open your eyes and look at me now."

I slowly lifted my lids, though they were not at all heavy. The smoke was thick and Chon was staring me in the face from a distance of not more than twelve inches. As the waves of copal smoke passed across his countenance, I clearly saw a greenish-yellow light within each of his eyes and I had a view of the fine bone structure beneath his skin. I gasped.

"OK, OK! That's all right," he said reassuringly. "Now stand up, Merlina. I want you to do the breath again. There is a channel, like a tube or a straw that runs from the center of will in the front, to a corresponding place in the back. Just shoot the energy through there with one strong inhale and an abdominal inward push. Then pull the energy up your back again. You can keep it going around and around this way.

When the energy gets up to the area behind your heart, let some of it branch off into your arms and hands. They'll heat up and magnetize. These are what you'll slice and work with.

"When the energy gets up to the back of your throat, change the quality of your breath. Push the energy up the back sinuses with a forceful exhale through the nostrils that originates as an inward push from the diaphragm. This breath will keep your field pumped up, hard and less penetrable, like a bicycle tire filled with just the right amount of air."

The channel in my umbilical region was open and it was quite easy to follow his instructions. My arms and hands filled as if molten magnetized gas were pouring into them. The breath he recommended for the back of the throat, which he also demonstrated, sounded very like a respirator, or the sound one hears underwater, tank breathing while scuba diving. Applying the breath as he suggested, I began to feel a weightless quality, almost as if I were a gas balloon filling. The tendency was to rock a little from side to side.

"Good!" he said. "Bend each knee as you lean to one side and then the other. Open those legs up and let them fill. Feel the energy start to rush in from the ground on the inhale and from above on the exhale. Now, when the serpent energy flowing up your spine reaches the top of your head, let the snake's mouth point to the zenith and let the mouth open. The serpent will begin to swallow energy from the cosmos. It will digest the energy and send it to all of your organs and senses to support your work. The overflow will be directed with your intent through your hands. This predigested cosmic energy converted into healing life force, this overflow, is the energy you will feed to the energy body of your patient. Think of it as cosmic baby food."

I had to laugh with glee.

"Yes!" Chon said. "Life is good! Fill with joy and love of life! Let these soothing qualities form like a coating of pearl, flowing down your liquid side as you work. Let the overflow relax and stabilize your patient. Keep the breath going around and around. Now, let me show you how to go in. Extend your right hand alongside of mine. Keep your field pumped up so that the magnetic flow entering the patient's energy field stops at your wrist."

Chon cuffed his right wrist by wrapping the thumb and index finger of his left hand around it to demonstrate what he meant. He had me do the same with my own hand so I could get the idea.

"The energy of your patient travels no farther to you than here," he repeated, emphasizing the wrist again. "Under no circumstances be a sponge and soak it up."

At that moment Pacha appeared in the doorway with the bucket of hot coals that Chon had requested. Chencha followed, carrying a large bowl of wintergreen alcohol. They placed the bucket on the ground at our feet and moved the small table near us. Chencha set the bowl of alcohol upon it. "If the energy needs to be discharged from the hands," Chon went on, "never fling it. Exit the patient's field gently. Place your hands into the alcohol and then shoot the drops like lightning from the fingertips directly into the bucket of burning embers. If you do it right, the fire will brighten." He demonstrated and fire leapt from the coals to consume the alcohol drops.

"Quite dramatic," I remarked.

"Also very effective," he replied.

The two girls looked on in amazement, then gazed at one another and scurried off to do more chores. I tried the hand-cleansing technique. The fire was present as the purifying forge of the Earth, and when it responded to the energy cast into it, it was a very welcome presence indeed.

"Now let me show you how to slice," Chon said. "Take your right hand and make a smooth vertical incision in the field, one smooth stroke. Then, using the left hand as well, spread the incision apart on the horizontal plane. To enter, go in gently, like a warm knife into cool butter. Insert the whole hand, fingertips first, with all the fingers compressed together, never spread. Try to insert them like a smooth dive enters the water. Make no ripples or splashes in the energy. When you exit, you'll do so in exactly the same manner, but in reverse.

"If you feel inclined to circulate the energy once you're inside the field, always do so in gentle clockwise turns. After the field has been opened, the further back you stand the more fine-tuned will be the bands of energy flow. If you stand close up they will be more diffuse, like a cloud. Keep this in mind as you work. Allow depleted areas to fill. Circulate stagnant areas and allow them to drain. Cleanse the hands as needed. The body will know what is required. To seal the field after you have exited, lift up from the bottom with both hands and then pour the energy over the patient's head, using a simultaneous hand motion downwards from each side until you reach the shoulder blades. Touching lightly there, the tips of your fingers resting momentarily on the top of each shoulder, let the patient shoulder the responsibility until their next treatment. Always gaze directly into their eyes at this moment with a silent mind, and convey a mental message, such as 'I am healing' or 'I am healed' if you sense that moment has arrived.

"You are just learning, Merlina, but if you had a long Dreaming association with many plants as I do, then they would also speak to you during the session, letting you know if they could be of service and if so, how. As it is, the patient's body will speak. You are a very good listener, Merlina, one of the best. Follow the flow. Listen to what you are told and do everything your body guides you to do."

"Even after having seen you work," I exclaimed with awe, "and having experienced your work, there is so much more to this than I ever imagined." I was absolutely overflowing with perceptual input.

"The unusual thing about healing," Chon said, "is that it shields itself from our view so that it may happen. The actual process seems invisible. We see befores and afters. Even if you watch a wound heal, you'll never actually see it. If you watch like a hawk for changes, you may see some of them, but not the process in all of its detail. Good healers know this, and so even though they are aware of what they are doing, they allow much of it to be invisible to the eye. This perhaps makes it confounding to the mind of the patient, but the major dose of energy thereby becomes totally accessible to the body and the healing systems. The veil is necessary, you see. The energies are shy and delicate.

"So, a good healer will always include something for the mind as well, such as a ceremony, or a purification that can be seen and felt. That way, the mind does not feel cheated and will not as easily attempt to sabotage the process. But remember, Merlina, the real work is subtle as a whisper and goes on invisibly. Only the trained eye can get even a fleeting glimpse of the energy body that moves with the speed and knowledge and grace of light."

Four patients arrived during the course of the morning and early afternoon. Chon requested that I energetically scan each one of them and then report my findings to him. He would follow up with his own scan, during which he worked on them himself and allowed me to observe. Following this, if herbs, dietary, or behavioral changes were required, he would spend time discussing his recommendations. At the end of each session he performed a *limpia*, a ceremony of energetic cleansing that was never repeated exactly the same way twice.

Chon instructed me in various methods of doing the limpia. One method which I like very much includes an energetic sweep of the field with a palm frond dipped in aromatic alcohol or a Mayan corn liquor called "posh." The alcohol spirits must be distilled pure and powerfully in order to drive away any unwanted energies. During the limpia, one literally rakes and washes the luminous fibers of the energy body using the frond as a sort of broom, and then as a palm fan or a wind machine to revive the spirit of the patient with strong gusts and tingling splashes of the aromatic liquid. While performing this limpia I can actually see the fire of the recipient's energy body burning more brightly and cleanly, as though I were feeding the fire with oxygen. I can also visually discern the beneficial effect upon the luminous fibers, which straighten and ripple during the cleansing, like long, luxuriant hair being brushed.

Chon has as many limpias as there are trees in the highlands. Another one of my favorites, which I love to watch him perform, is a fire limpia. The dramatic effect of this cleansing is peerless, and Chon sometimes uses it for spiritual maladies and against witchcraft. During the limpia Chon will take a swig of posh, but not swallow. With a lit candle in front of his mouth he forcefully sprays droplets of posh from his pursed lips. The spray naturally ignites when touched by the flame of the candle and Chon will continue gracefully following the contours and outline of the patient's energy body until he has completed a full sweep. He says that there are certain types of energies that cling to our energy bodies and that these energies do not like the burning sensation of alcohol, salt water or flame, any of which can be used in a cleansing, with a spray from the mouth. Chon has shown me how to do the spitting, which, when performed correctly, comes out as forcefully as though propelled by an aerosol can. I can even ignite the spray, but I have never felt the confidence or perhaps the sheer audacity, coupled with the necessary control, to aim the flaming blast at anybody. Chon performs this feat as casually as one might whistle a merry tune. He jokes and says that the serpent has to age before it can breathe fire with impunity.

As afternoon wore on, after the fourth patient had been seen and had left, Chon announced that he was through for the day and that he, don Juan, and doña Celestina would be leaving the house for a while to attend to some business in town. Chon asked me if I would remain, just in case someone else showed up. He instructed me that in such an event, if they had come for a scan I should give them one. I agreed with quite a sense of trepidation, still trusting that Chon knew what he was doing.

About an hour after they had gone, there was in fact a knock at the front gate. Not even the young women seemed to be around to answer it, so I went myself. Wondering who it might be and for what purpose, I got quite a shock when I opened the front door. I was surprised to see Carlo Castillo, a former apprentice and long-time acquaintance of don Juan, Chon, and doña Celestina who had fallen out of favor years ago and had not been received by them since. I myself had not seen Carlo in a number of years due to the breach in their association.

I must have just stared in silence for a moment. Carlo looked back at me with amusement. His appearance was radically altered since our last encounter. Formerly quite robust, Carlo was now almost emaciated with the stooped shoulders of a broken old man. His hair, which had been wavy, lustrous, and black, was now completely gray, brittle, and uncombed. His left eye appeared to have ruptured a blood vessel behind the iris, or perhaps was developing a cataract. He was dressed nicely though, in dark slacks, a matching shirt, and a tan jacket.

"Expecting someone else?" he tried to joke defiantly with a half smile.

I couldn't help but notice then that his teeth were false. "Carlo!" I said with astonishment. "What are you trying to do? You know they'll never see you."

"Actually," he said, "I was hoping for you."

I remembered Chon's instructions. "I can let you in for a moment," I replied. "I was working in the back." I suggested that we talk there in the hopes of an opportunity to scan his energy body and see what was going on.

He followed me like a puppy through a house with which he had once been somewhat familiar. When we reached the back room, he looked through the doorway.

"So this is what you are learning now?" he asked.

I pulled out two chairs for us so that we could sit in the mild afternoon sunlight.

"Among other things," I conceded. I put my hand on his left shoulder. He seemed to welcome the gentle touch. "Would you mind if I had a look at you? I'm not as proficient as Chon, mind you, but I See something going on."

"Fire away," he said and slipped off his jacket, hanging it on the chair back.

I silenced my mind and took a deep breath, focusing on the balanced dispassion I had been developing in this place to assist me in my work. The last thing that could help either of us would be for me to be flooded with too many strong emotions. I placed my hands into his energy field at the left shoulder blade front and back and proceeded to scan his left side.

The eye was definitely out of focus and there was an impairment to hearing in the ear. When I reached the throat, I said "You talk too much." It was involuntary, as though I were speaking to myself, but he heard me and I felt his body shake a bit with silent laughter. I sensed something in the heart area, anger or perhaps sadness. I verbalized this.

"How about a combination?" he responded sarcastically.

When I got to the spleen area, there was a definite indication that it was being severely overworked and depleting. I circulated the energy there and he seemed to recognize the value of this. I scanned the left adrenal, which was in working order, perhaps even overactive and compensating for a breakdown elsewhere.

A move to the right side yielded the reason. I began to see black clouds around the organs and the emotions. The liver was definitely malfunctioning. He was not yellow, so it was not jaundice. "There is a problem here," I said gently, circulating my hand around the liver area.

"That's the one," he said and looked up at me with a little amazement. His eyes were a bit watery.

I finished the scan of his right side, sealed the energy and pulled up my chair to sit down by him. "Do you want to tell me about it?"

"Cancer," he remarked flatly.

I had no emotional response, and yet I knew that I cared more than words could express. I reminded myself that this was the appropriate position to be in energetically, if I was going to do my work. "What are you doing for it?" I asked.

"What I can," he said dryly.

"I could offer you some advice, but I doubt that you would accept it. Is there anything that I might do to help you?"

"Who knows?" he said. "Thank you. I mean that. You are very kind." He sighed and looked at me longingly. "I suppose that I just wanted to see you again. I thought you might understand."

"I do, Coyol," I said softly, calling him by the nickname Chon and I had for him, and tousling his hair.

He looked at me with curiosity and more than a little hope. "I guess I'd better go before I'm handed my hat." He rose from his chair, smoothed his slacks, and put on his jacket.

I nodded and walked him to the gate.

"You know I'd love to see you again. Any chance of you moving back out this way?" he asked as he stood in the street.

"I already have, but the only time I've seen my apartment was to move a few things into it." I smiled.

"Yes." he said somberly. "I remember how that is."

"Goodbye, Carlo," I said to him.

"Goodbye," he said cheerfully, and smiled.

As I walked back to the patio, I knew that Chon had provided me with an opportunity to be alone with Carlo. Later Chon would say that it is really the patient, and not the healer, who is the miracle worker. Some choose life and some do not, but the universe is a mystery either way.

PRACTICE TWELVE

ENERGY SCANNING

1. Perform one circulation of fire breath (see pages 93–4).
2. On the second round, as you move energy up the spine to the back heart area, keep the arms relaxed and let the energy branch out from the heart to fill the arms and hands with magnetized heat. Feel pulsing, moisture, or a tingling sensation form in the palms and fingers. Maintain the arms relaxed with the fingers softly curled.
3. Continue bringing the energy up the back with fire breath, finally activating the inner eye by breathing through the back sinuses. Then tip the head slightly to transfer the energy through the forehead to the liquid side of the body. (Chon calls the front the liquid side, because the majority of gland and organ fluids are formed in the front.)
4. Breathe down the front side of the body, using abdominal expansion on the inhale, until the energy reaches the heart area and again floods the arms and hands with warmth, and this time, the additional, soft, caressing feeling of love.
5. The first exercise to develop sensitized, healing hands is to use the breath again in order to pump up the energy field around them. Using a moderately forceful exhale through the back throat, back sinuses, and nostrils, combined with an abdominal contraction, pump the air out. The sound this breath makes is reminiscent of a bicycle pump. This will fuel the fire of your energy field.

6. Now, test the magnetized sensation of your hands by slowly raising them, still keeping them relaxed with fingers softly curled. Gently move them towards one another until you feel them repel like identical poles of two magnets. Use the pumping breath to increase the size of your field and build up the distance between the palms.

   The greater the distance you can maintain before feeling the palms repel, the greater will be the capacity of your palms to sense irregularities during a scan and to move the energy in a corrective, balancing fashion.

7. Practice often. When you wish to return the energy, follow the rest of the process for completing fire breath, bringing the energy all the way down the front of the body, to be stored in the center of will.

THE FEMALE
ORGASMIC
PRACTICES

I SPENT THE REST OF THE AFTERNOON AND EVENING ALONE in doña Celestina's home. When no one returned by dinner, I heated some chicken tamales and served them smothered with pumpkin seed mole sauce. I felt that everyone was intentionally giving me some time to be alone, so after dinner I listened to Mozart on a National Public Radio broadcast from Yuma and then went to bed.

I was awakened by a knock at my bedroom door at about 4 in the morning. Having turned in early the previous night, I was not at all startled by the knock. I ran my fingers through my hair and opened the door to find doña Celestina standing there, fully dressed.

"Put on your robe and come to my garden," she whispered.

I slipped a dusk-colored silk dressing gown over my nightgown and followed her through the passageway, turning right down the little hall before reaching the waiting area of her consultation room. She unlocked a wooden door at the end of the small hallway and I saw that it opened onto her enclosed private garden. A very fragrant night-blooming flower abounded there. The air was heady with large white trumpeting blossoms opened to the moonlight, which she called "florifundio."

I was also immediately aware of the presence of many huge flying moths. They flitted and sputtered everywhere. We tiptoed along a tiny path that led to a mesh nursery of sorts, larger than a bird house but smaller than a dovecote, where, thanks to the moonlight, I could make out many cocoons in various stages of development attached to the sides of the mesh. There were quite a few large, moist, partially chewed leaves at the bottom of the construction, which appeared to have served as food for the larvae or the emerging adult. I remembered having read that many moths like nightshade and I looked around to see if any was about, noticing only the florifundio. I also noticed that something which looked very like honey had been applied to some leaves that were stuck into the mesh, and also to some of those sitting half-eaten at the bottom of the nursery.

"What kind of moths are they?" I asked.

"Come and have a look," she whispered and led me to a bush where a very large moth sat resting, wings opened.

It was glorious—beautiful buttery vanilla ice cream with caramel swirls for colors, and large eye designs on the wings, which when opened were as massive as the palm of my hand. I crooned.

"She's letting you get very close," doña Celestina said. "See if you can touch her, but not on the wings. Touch her underside. That's what she'll like."

I extended the tip of my ring finger to softly stroke her furry, bulbous underbody. Her hair was thick and soft, like shaved ermine. The touch seemed pleasurable to her and she moved her body rhythmically back and forth to meet the tip of my finger.

"That's enough," doña Celestina said. "We don't want to bother her. We just want to say hello."

"This garden is beautiful at night," I remarked in earnest praise, drinking in the luminosity of the silvery, milky light that seemed to rest like dew on the surface of every living thing within it.

"I thought you would appreciate it," doña Celestina whispered. "This is my private place, where I come for a recharge."

"It's magical!" I exclaimed, almost wanting to dance among the flowers, the moths, and the moonlight.

"I brought you here because healing work, although it circulates and feeds the sexual energies, can sometimes sap them a bit. I want to teach you some personal practices that are very private, sensual, abundant, and sublime like my garden here, practices that are just for women."

Doña Celestina motioned toward a place on the ground where I could see fired clay tiles, creating a space large enough for sitting, set not far from a simple earthen bird basin and many flowering florifundio. We sat cross-legged on the tiles facing each other, and folding our garments underneath us.

"I'm going to speak candidly," she began.

"Very well," I said.

"I'm a grown woman. I've no time for prudery. We're going to deepen the topic of the female orgasm."

"What, do you mean Chon didn't want to teach me this?" I giggled.

She smiled back in her sly way, teeth glinting in the moonlight. "You just wait. Juan is going to talk with you about the men."

I gulped. That got to me. The mood was not one of whispered secrets in the wee hours. I humbly realized that I did not even know everything about my own body's responses, much less the capabilities of another gender, and that I was about to acquire life knowledge.

"Women are different from men," doña Celestina said, "not just by virtue of the womb, but also in that they are capable of a series of multiple climaxes, without losing the energy from one to the next. If a woman knows what she is doing, she can pull on an energetic column within the center of her being and the sensations of energy will move upward, like going up a flight of stairs. It is possible for them to continue upward until they reach and fountain out of the top of her head, only to be recirculated again at the bottom of her pool of energy, and sent back up to the top.

"The waters of a woman's womb, as I told you in my altar room, are present if the woman has the capacity for orgasmic response. If she has lost that capacity, we say she is 'cracked,' like a broken vessel, because this energy center leaks. It is dried up, strained, and weak. Women must explore their own bodies and work through emotional traumas to rekindle their ability to reach climaxes of pleasure, if this possibility has been lost in them. As Chon has often told you, joy is soothing, balancing, and life-affirming. It strengthens the body for what it must endure, be it childbirth, hardship, old age, whatever. Many women who have lost their capacity for pleasure, and have lost the waters of the womb, instead reach climaxes of pain, which are life-denying and destructive, weakening to the forces, since they are unnecessary.

"A woman must recover her capacity for orgasm, not only once but consecutively. Too often we look to the men for our examples. In this case it should be the other way around. Once this multiple capacity has been found, a woman may then go on to what I will share with you now."

"Before you do, doña, what are the key points in working through emotional traumas? You are always able to concentrate issues into their essence." I was keenly interested in advice that she might have for women.

"First of all," she said, "recognize that male energy can be indolent. Some individuals just want to expel the sexual energies to relieve themselves of pressure. This angers the serpent in both males and females and can cause trauma. The serpent will shed skins and, over time, will turn such uses of male energy into a fat ogre or a wasted weakling, as it ages. On the other hand, many females withhold orgasmic responses out of manipulation, anger, or fear. This only cheats them, and with no waters they begin to shrivel from the inside out, or perhaps they remain emotional children. It would be far better for all to recognize these scenarios, end these relationships, and explore the pure nature of sexual energies, but often people remain in unfulfilling or even dangerous situations, in the hopes of material benefit, companionship, or protection. Their own strength and resourcefulness would be better served as their protector, provider, and companion, but perhaps they lack courage. They seek someone else to fulfill them. You have seen for yourself in my consultation where these situations can lead.

"To compound that, we now live in a male dominator society throughout most of the world and this also works its ills on both males, females, and their offspring. Couple that with the repression implemented by organized religions and government exploitation and you have a real mess. There are many steps to retrace."

"So, as with other practices of shamanism, in this day and age, the key is that we almost unlearn some of what we have learned and begin afresh," I paraphrased. "Surviving in nonconventional circumstances will strengthen and purify us, and deepens our wisdom, generating energy for us and allowing us to function in life through a healthy alternative."

"Exactly," the doña nodded, "but it's not always necessary to throw the baby out with the bath water. Some people, like shamans and wise women, never really agree with the status quo. Perhaps because of it they would not even survive, if not for some unseen power. That makes them desirable in times of need. They never totally buy into the world order, hook, line and sinker. You are one of those people, Merlina, and that is why you have so much freed energy to work with.

You are not entangled in believing in a system, nor are you locked into rebelling against one. You have tremendous energy, and fortunately for you it is not caught by things that do not work. This is an ideal situation. Such a position has much to offer female empowerment."

"Back to your practices," I said thoughtfully, "How does a woman pull her sexual responses into higher energy centers, and what is the purpose, other than the circulation of the energy?" I asked.

"Even if the purpose were only circulation, that would be enough," doña Celestina answered. "As Chon has told you, circulating the energy is cleansing, healing, and restorative. It releases blocks, fills depletions, and balances the being. There is more to it, however. First of all, a woman not only circulates energy, she can actually *generate* energy with orgasm. Remember that this energy is not lost, being expelled from the body, as is the case for the male. A woman retains orgasmic energy within the body. She must pull the energy upwards so that all the energy centers, the entire energy body in fact, reap the benefits. Otherwise this energy is wasted in another way, through imbalance, which can cause problems. One center will overfill and the others will go wanting, doing the work but receiving no replenishment. That is how a woman can exhaust herself. So you see, she must shift her focus and address all her energy centers. That is why I shifted mine and brought you here into my garden.

"This place has powerful sexual energy of a higher sort," she continued. "It is silvery and placental in the moonlight. The earth is cool. The night flowers are open, fragrant and blooming. And the moths . . . just look at them, pulsating, buzzing with energy, so lush and sensual!"

A very large Cecropia moth alighted near us.

"Observe the body," doña Celestina explained, pointing gently to the beautiful creature with a bent index finger.

The moth was perched at the tip of a florifundio blossom. It spread its wings and appeared to be resting there.

"Look at the wing span!" she whispered. "Her energy must fountain above the tips of her antennae and out to the sides, well beyond the breadth of her wings, and then return to her base to act as the generator for pumping those wings in flight. As a caterpillar she spun her cocoon from her lower sexual center, digesting leaves to feed it. Now she is purely highly sexual, the energy has been elevated. She eats less and the energy emerges from the higher centers rather than from the lower, to create her wings and flight!"

Doña Celestina's explanation of the life cycle of these moths was matchless. I was in awe observing them as they fluttered about in the light of the waning moon. "The woman's internal energy column is like the silk cord of the moths, then?" I volunteered.

"So it is!" she spoke emphatically. "They are speaking to you now. You have got a good dusting of their knowledge out here in these early hours. That same pulling and throbbing motion that a moth uses to emit her silken thread can also be used to pull the energy back in and up through the body, to come out of the head and fountain around our energetic wing span. Don Juan and Chon have already taught you the fire breath. For the orgasmic woman, the breath may be pulled up the central column rather than up the back. This is a difference present in the woman's orgasmic breath. One powerful inward breath, combined with one abdominal contraction and an upward pull on all of the internal muscles originating in the inner thighs, through the vagina and upwards, will lift the energy generation one rung on the ladder."

"Wow!" I felt silly at my own lack of eloquence, but that sound just exploded from my lips.

Doña Celestina controlled the desire to snicker at me. She demonstrated the breath and I followed her example, breathing energy up from the vaginal area with an inhale accompanied by an abdominal contraction, coupled with inner thigh, vaginal, and uterine contractions.

"You may wonder how an old Indian woman comes across knowledge like this," she smiled. "The fact is, as a young woman I first learned from a midwife. Many of the tools and magical implements that are on a witch's altar can also be found among the midwife's medicine bag, the knives, the water, the herbs, the knowledge of the time and place for various breaths, pushes, and muscle contractions . . . When I was a girl, Indian women in Mexico had to deliver without doctors. Most of the time they wouldn't even allow us in the hospitals if we were dying. In those cases sometimes a doctor would come to us. Villages had to have *curanderos* [healers], shamans, midwives, witches and the like in order to survive the normal hazards of life. We really did learn things that people don't seem to know today.

"During a girl's puberty initiation, for example, she would be taught not just about menstruation and reproduction but also about giving, receiving, and enhancing pleasure. She would then ingest either Datura or an alcohol extract of tobacco, and would sometimes also ingest a certain type of red ant that lives in these deserts. The initiate would experience visions and would have to bridge them, and if the women shamans present saw an omen about the girl, she would be taught female power and would apprentice with a healer, a midwife, or a witch. In my case I apprenticed at one time or another with all three. My special talent was, of course, for sorcery."

"Don Juan has told me about some of the male initiation sites in the area. Do the women still have sites as well, doña Celestina?" I asked with great curiosity.

"Oh, yes. It is really too bad that you do not have this in your culture. Perhaps this is something the circle of women should begin. We do have sites, rattlesnake caves and pillar stones. I'll even take you to one. There you'll see the red hand-prints of many female initiates, red for the menstrual blood and power, and red rattlesnake motifs painted by young women such as myself, who succeeded in Seeing the rat-tlesnake spirit and received some of the power. Once we have finished your instruction, before we let you return to Yuma for a while, I'll take you there myself. For now, though, we are going to saturate you with knowledge, while we have all three of your teachers in one place, staying here in my home. Do you have any questions about the women's applications of fire breath?"

"Can the woman's breath be used at other times or only during sexual arousal?" I asked.

"It is always used during arousal, but it's important to know that arousal doesn't necessarily mean human inter-course, or even some kind of consensual act between human partners. One may feel sexually aroused and potentiated by the forces of nature. Women, for example, can have inter-course with fire, or the steaming water of a cauldron, or with the wind. All that need be done is to breathe the energy in. Allow it to enter into the body. When sensations begin, when the serpent begins to awaken, fire up the energy with the breath and pull it upward, center by center. Women do not need men, or even acts of self-excitation for their sexual satis-faction. The elements and forces will provide this if a woman is sensual enough. Also remember that sexual responses that are circulated through all the centers with the fire breath actu-ally generate energy for the female. This is most important. She can increase and replenish her energy through her sexual response. That is the core of the message, but it must be accomplished properly and with the right intent. Simply engaging in wanton intercourse will not increase energy. It will only increase appetite."

I laughed.

"The sun will be up soon," doña Celestina said. "Perhaps you would like a steamy shower and a nice hot cup of ephedra before breakfast."

"Thank you for sharing your garden and your knowledge with me, doña," I said, rising to go. "This is something I'll never forget."

"I hope not," she replied, "because Juan has some tall tales for you later today! If you practice the breath, Merlina, the energies will never forget you either."

I raised my eyebrows with interest, smiling at the thought, and pushed the wooden door open.

PRACTICE THIRTEEN

FEMALE ORGASMIC BREATH

1. This breath is similar to fire breath. Rather than pulling the energy up the back and down the front, it is pulled up the central energy column within the body and fountains out of the top of the head. Then it flows around the sides and collects again in a pool at the starting point, to be brought back up over and over.

2. Begin by squeezing and pulling up on the vaginal and inner thigh muscles. Combine this action with a powerful inhale through the nostrils, which is accompanied by an abdominal contraction.

3. Continue this breathing and movement and attempt to activate upward uterine contractions, while pulling up on all the reproductive muscles. (This movement is good for positioning the uterus properly within the body, and for counteracting the effects of gravity and menstruation. The flow pulls energy into the uterus through the vagina, rather than expelling energy from it. If menstruating, do the breath lying on your back.)

4. Now lift the energy and sensation into the diaphragm and then up into the heart area. Use powerful in breaths accompanied by upward pulls on the diaphragm and abdominal contractions. Continue all the previous steps, adding these movements to them.

5. Inhale through the back sinuses and combine an abdominal contraction and upward push. This will pull the energy up from the heart into the inner eye. From there, with continued inhales, during which all of these steps are combined at once, the energy will fountain out of the top of the head. The exhales now should be ones of deep satisfaction and release. The energy will flow to your sides at about an arm's length or more, and will then collect in a pool below you, to be brought back up once again.

The Male
Sexual Energy

LATER THAT DAY, DON JUAN AMBLED OUT INTO THE patio rubbing his cheeks and jaws with his large hands, as if suppressing a big smile. He had on his straw hat to hide the mischievous glint in his eyes and I knew that I was in for it.

I decided that the only way to survive was to be open about my feelings. "I must admit that I'm a bit apprehensive about our time together this afternoon, don Juan," I said with a smile, half joking and at the same time quite serious.

He burst out laughing, which was the first and the last thing I needed. "Why?" he asked with mock concern. "You don't think I'm going to talk dirty to you, do you?"

I heard Chon's cackling from the kitchen.

"Come on, Merlina. You know me better than that," he joked.

"I'm not so sure," I replied. "Some of your stories can get pretty wild." Chon continued his guffawing and stuck his head out from the kitchen to wink at me.

"Now that you remind me," don Juan pondered, stroking his lower jaw, "I do have just the perfect tale." He feigned amazement as though an ingenious idea had just dawned on him out of nowhere. "We'd better take a ride in the desert," he

140

advised. "I don't want to burn Chon's ears. And I promise I won't start talking until we get there. Otherwise, you might crash the car and kill us both!" He held his side as he struggled to hold back his laughter.

It was hopeless and I knew it. Chon was hysterical and don Juan just stood there grinning at me. He extended his arm to me and there was nothing I could do but oblige and go with him, or perhaps hide in my room, in which case I was sure I'd be served up for supper. I accepted my fate.

He slapped me between the shoulder blades and bade me welcome. "Don't worry, Merlina, you won't be in the least prudish by the time I get through with you. Even if you think that you're already in the know, I'm going to tell you how sorcerers satisfy their women! I may even show you!"

At that, I heard something non-breakable hit the floor in the kitchen. No doubt Chon was doubled over with laughter until well after we had driven away. The ride into the desert proved to be no consolation, especially when don Juan began to entertain me with maxims like, "I have always felt women are rather like cats who don't want to be bothered unless they come nosing around." The truth of the matter is that I doubted my ability to discern when he was being serious and when he was offering one of his keen parodies of human behavior. I guessed that I would just have to pray and trust my power.

Perhaps to settle me, don Juan asked me to drive in a southerly direction through the Sonoran desert until we reached the Gulf of Santa Clara, some fifty kilometers from San Luis. We both loved the Gulf, with its warm, clean, calm waters and mysteriously deep tides, some of the most extreme on Earth, retreating in places almost a mile from the high mark.

The Gulf of Santa Clara is essentially pristine and almost completely deserted, surrounded by desert terrain, cacti and salt water-loving mesquite. It is the northerly starting point of the Sea of Cortez, the waters of which are teaming with four species of whale during the winter season, giant sea turtles, marlin, and giant blue prawns, which rank among the most delicious in the world.

I was quite exhilarated by the time we arrived, having long forgotten any nervousness, and was looking forward to spending a day at the beach. We parked the jeep on a solitary stretch of beautiful shoreline and unloaded two straw mats that don Juan had stowed in the back. After a short walk we found the perfect spot to relax and unrolled the mats on the soft sand. The sun was quite mild, so we took off our hats, rolled up our slacks and walked in silence for a quarter mile or so. Don Juan enjoyed walking silently at the shore; whenever we went to nearby beaches, if we stayed overnight he would invariably rise before dawn in order to "receive the energy patterns of the new day," and would then spend the first moments after sunup quietly raking them into the sand with a dry palm frond.

We returned to our straw mats thoroughly refreshed after our walk, and relaxed back, putting our hats over our eyes. Don Juan began the discourse casually, with a matter-of-fact manner.

"You've probably noticed that there are slightly fewer males born into the world than there are females," he said lightheartedly. "Men have often misinterpreted this. Because we are slightly more scarce, we elevate our own importance. Increased value is not the reason for our reduced numbers, however. It only takes one good male to populate, providing that there are many women."

I snickered under my hat.

"Women are the necessary element," he went on. "They begin the whole process by bringing the male into existence. Diverse strong males and females mean a strong species. Males have a competitive streak, because, as I said, it takes good ones.

We rank one another according to our own criteria for health, strength, courage, intelligence, and integrity. However, the criteria used by women are different and include not only these factors, but also others, not the least of which is sexual potency. Longevity, for example, is directly related to potency in males and is a highly desirable characteristic."

"So what you mean by potency in no way refers to sexual conquests. Am I right, don Juan?" I asked, relieved that I had my hat to cover my face.

"Let me address that topic for you at length," he laughed. "At our first peak, as very young men, we practically ulcerate for sexual attention and relations. I myself was strong and fit, and very foolhardy, I might add. I actually stole a young woman to be my bride from a neighboring tribe, which was a common practice among many Native groups during my youth. I was so obsessed by my desire that I didn't even notice she had recently given birth until I had her with me. By the time I could return her, the infant had died. Naturally, being a forceful fellow I took the consequences of my actions very hard. I realized that there is powerful force behind sexual energy and sought to become wise regarding its uses.

"One of my first mentors was a rattlesnake shaman. He taught me that, though the serpent will often bite, it does not always expel its venom, and that this in part accounts for its longevity and wisdom. Through observing rattlesnakes with my benefactor I learned how they enter into a relaxed trance state by rolling their eyes up into the back of their heads. By focusing on the top of my head in this fashion, and by pulling the sexual energies and fluids up through the body of the serpent, up through my spine, I was able to ascertain the secret of the 'dry bite.'

"You see, for a man, the mouth of the serpent becomes the genitals and the head is the rattle. By sipping back on the sexual energies and fluids, using fire breath up the spine, accompanied by a roll of the eyes deep into the back of the head, rather than by expelling the energy, one increases the number of rattles on the tail; one increases longevity, always indicated by the length of the rattle, and wisdom, indicated by its shake, the stimulation.

"Men do not have limitless sexual energies, despite what we may wish our partners to believe. One way to tell if a male is endowed with abundant sexual energy is, of course, to have intercourse with him, but a woman should never allow herself to conceive, if pregnancy is her desire, until after she has ascertained this, among other aspects of her criteria.

"A male with ample energies will be able to demonstrate them all night, without expelling the energies. The next day he will be energized, even though he has not slept. Neither will he fall into a death slumber afterwards, if the energies are released for conception, and when they are, conception will almost invariably occur if the couple is mindful of all the essentials. The act will be pleasurable and always evolve, exploring new territory. It will not become dull and repetitive.

"For these reasons, when a man is in young adulthood it is wiser if he views these energies to be the treasures that they are. We are given a limited quantity for a reason, to focus upon quality. The fact that a male can discharge power during intercourse, rather than exclusively generate power, as with the orgasmic female, should cause him to be mindful. Like females, who can be endowed with much natural wisdom in these areas, the adult male should concentrate upon generating and circulating the sexual energy, for passion and pleasure, vigorous longevity, and vital well-being.

"Doña Celestina has told you that a woman need not engage in sexual relations with a human partner in order to have pleasure and circulate the energies. Rather, she may engage energies directly . . . fire, steaming water, the wind. Once a male has aged and practiced rattlesnake wisdom sufficiently, like an old serpent, he may snort the energies up into his spine, to the top of his head, without engaging in any type of human intercourse or stimulation. This is his second peak. He may also engage external energies directly, providing he has practiced sufficiently and understands the difference between energetic union and penile penetration.

"We'll discuss that topic at more length another time, but for now let me point out that it is possible to have energetic intercourse."

"Is that anything like ritual intercourse, or like a shaman and his sacred cave?" I asked, intrigued.

"Not like the first, but somewhat like the second," don Juan replied, chuckling softly. I knew I was in for a story. "Do you remember how a sorceress determines her affinity with a particular direction of the wind?" he asked in a coy tone.

How could I forget! In this ceremony, practiced by Sonoran desert shamans, the initiate, in this case a female, hikes to a deserted spot on a completely windless day. This spot must be frequented by wind from all four directions, and not have one or more directions that are predominant. There she strips naked and lies spread-eagle on a smooth boulder, face up. She must remain until a wind is excited and blows over her. The direction from which the wind comes is her most favorable direction, and if a small twister kicks up, then she has an affinity with all four, which was my case.

After approximately four hours of lying exposed on a rather fresh desert afternoon some years ago, with don Juan waiting about a quarter-mile away, politely out of sight, I experienced the whirlwind coming to me. I had undertaken the ceremony so that don Juan could convince me of its effectiveness. After the response from the wind, which included sensations of it tickling my stomach and actually trying to get into my body, I must admit I was completely convinced.

"Yes . . ." I replied, somewhat suspicious of the theme.

"Well," he said. "In order to do what I'm going to tell you about, in addition to knowing a woman's winds one must have the double, the energy body, and be able to move it at will, without configuring it into a form. Some practitioners choose to move their energy bodies as wind."

"What?" I exclaimed.

"I knew a sorcerer who could perform such a maneuver," don Juan justified with a nod of his head. "He had a reputation for terrorizing his female apprentices, but no one could really figure out how he was doing it, since the girls had always been alone, before running into town half-naked screaming with fright."

"Go on," I coaxed him.

"This sorcerer, whose name was Melquior Ángelo, would characteristically present each one of his 'winds,' young female apprentices he would attract, with a blanket, hand-woven, each one distinctive. The women always accepted such a valuable and useful gift as a sign of prestige, and as a covenant between sorcerer and apprentice. Melquior would counsel them that if they wished to be imbued with power, they need only lie and sleep naked upon the blanket.

"Naturally, each one greedily tried it, hoping to be converted instantly into a sorceress of renown, or a deity of beauty and power. What happened next was a mystery, but they always experienced fear afterwards, and would quickly leave the village, sometimes disappearing within weeks. No villager could figure out what was happening to the women after receiving the blanket, or imagine how this gift could possibly terrify them so or cause them to run away. Yet it was always afterwards that the girls vanished. No bodies were ever found, so Melquior could not really be accused of anything, and still young women clamored for this sorcerer's attentions, since of course his reputation was rapidly growing.

"Finally one day, a young woman came running into town

naked after having received a blanket. She was screaming at the top of her lungs."

"How did she explain herself?" I asked.

"She screamed that she was being fucked by the wind," don Juan said dramatically. "Her family and friends grabbed her and tried to calm her down and put some clothes on her. Together they all walked back to her house, where they found nothing unusual but Melquior's blanket spread out on the floor of her altar room."

"Hmm! Well . . . what happened to the girl?" I asked with great curiosity, sitting up and lifting my hat from my face.

"Oh, she moved away to live with her aunt in another village. Like the others, she turned up elsewhere later," don Juan remarked casually.

"No, don Juan. You can't leave it like that! I mean what 'happened' to her. What did she experience?" I insisted.

"Why Melquior, of course," he said covering a large smirk on his face by readjusting his hat and then folding his hands over his chest as he continued to recline. "His energy body was attached to those blankets, like a breeze blowing around it, and when the women unrolled the blankets and lay down upon them naked, well . . . I don't think I need to elaborate more."

I laughed out loud at the audacity of the maneuver. "And what pleasure could he possibly get from that, assuming that he terrified them all half to death?"

"Oh . . . excitation, and just good sport," don Juan chuckled knowingly. "Ideally, though, he would have found someone who enjoyed it and could harness the energy."

I covered a smirk on my face with my hand. "Oh. Yes, ideally so. Well, I knew I was in for wild stories with you, don Juan, but I have to admit this one exceeds my expectations," I teased.

"Never give someone only what they expect," he remarked in a tantalizing voice. "What satisfaction is there in that?"

PRACTICE FOURTEEN

RATTLESNAKE BREATH

1. This breath is another variation of fire breath, which pulls the energy up the spine and into the top of the head. It may be used by men for seminal retention, or by women and men for longevity and wisdom. Visualize an openmouthed rattlesnake. The mouth is your genital area; the body, your spine. The rattle is rooted in your inner eye and, as the serpent ages, it will lengthen. (In advanced practitioners the rattle will sometimes emerge from an opening at the central top of the forehead, near the hairline.)

2. Perform fire breath up the back, pulling the energy through all the spinal centers, using forceful inhales through the nostrils and abdominal contractions. Keep the body relaxed. Do not stiffen or tense the body in any way. (In men, bodily rigidity, especially in the legs, is often a precursor to ejaculation.) Use the sheer force of the inhales to move energy upward.

3. As the energy reaches the heart area, roll the eyes up and back into the skull. Continue the inhales and abdominal contractions. Concentrate on inhaling with the back sinuses as the energy rises from the spine and floods the inner eye, located near the pineal gland.

4. The energy will climax by becoming erect and vibrating or rattling the pineal, which will open the inner eye when you are ready. This shaking of the pineal releases pleasure, well-being, and a wisdom-enhancing elixir into the brain.

THE
CELESTIAL WASH

ON OUR RETURN FROM THE GULF OF SANTA CLARA, don Juan and I stopped at a local vendor and purchased several kilos of giant blue prawns. Doña Celestina oversaw their preparation, demonstrating to her girls the proper method of cleaning, and requesting them simmered in coconut milk and green chile, served with steamed chayote, a small, succulent green squash with a large, soft, edible seed.

As we sat down at the patio dining table, such a ferocious wind kicked up that we had to move the meal into the kitchen and eat at the cozy wooden table in front of the gas stove. The kitchen was warmed by the glow of kerosene lanterns reflecting off the blue-and-white Puebla tiles and softly whitewashed walls. We made ourselves comfortable at the lively hand-painted dinette, as the wind whistled and howled, blowing dust throughout the patio.

"There'll be thunder and lightning, but no rain until very late tonight," Chon commented, sniffing the air as he rolled up a corn tortilla filled with prawns and sauce.

"I think the 'wind' is looking for Merlina. It's a good thing we moved inside, or we'd never be able to finish our food," don Juan teased.

Everyone laughed and I endured poking and jokes about the "wind" all through supper. Doña Celestina suggested that now might be the time for me to hide in my room, as if she had been reading my thoughts of earlier that day, saying that she needed me fresh for all the work we were going to do, and not worn out from a sleepless night with the "wind."

Despite their endless charades and antics, and all our laughter, I managed to eat my goodly portion of the delicious meal, and determined to sleep afterwards, retiring to my room while they were still hooting. My sleep was continually disturbed throughout the night by the rattling of the wind at my door and the moaning sound of it blowing underneath, through the doorwell. This racket was occasionally punctuated by loud banging, which would startle me, almost levitating a few inches above my bed for a moment, as the door visibly shook before my eyes with the force of an invisible blow. This would be followed by the sound of Chon's cackling, or don Juan's hysterical laughter coming through the walls. It was quite a challenging night.

When finally there was a human knock at the door, I almost didn't answer it. Only the sound of doña Celestina's laughter on the other side convinced me to get out of bed.

When I finally peeked through the door, she was standing there with a candle in her hand.

"Cuando toca la Pelona, no se abre," she said. (When old woman death knocks, one doesn't open.)

"Ni para el viento abro," I responded. (Neither do I open for the wind.)

She doubled over with laughter, holding on to her candle with one hand and to the back of a nearby chair for support with the other.

When I had splashed my face and put on my dressing gown, I joined her outside on the patio. The wind seemed to still and a soft warm drizzle began to fall. The sensation of the gentle warm drops tapping on my head and running down my neck was so relaxing after the night's bumpy ride, that all of a sudden I experienced an all over bodily shudder, which began at my head and rushed all the way down to my toes and into the earth. It felt as though someone had opened the top of my head and poured warm-scented oil through my body. The sensation was ecstatic, most pleasurable, and caught my abdomen with the thrill one experiences from a soft dip on a roller coaster.

I have at times experienced such a feeling listening to moving poetry or music, or viewing a magnificent work of art or an awesome natural spectacle of beauty, but never have I had such a feeling standing in the rain at night, seemingly devoid of most visual and auditory sensations, and yet filled to the brim with them.

Doña Celestina held the candlelight up to my eyes and examined them a long time, looking within my pupils. "That's good," she said. "It would be a shame for the wind to do all that work for nothing. Let's sit down in the rocking chairs and enjoy this warm, caressing rain."

I was quite amenable to her suggestion, warmed by it in fact, and made myself comfortable in one of the bentwood rockers. She did the same a short distance across from me, rocking in silence. Rocking was almost hypnotic, lulling me into a sensation of protection, of comfort and ease I hadn't had since I was a child, and had experienced very seldom even then.

"I call that shuddering sensation you felt the celestial wash," she remarked softly. "It is a response of the energy body to something that thrills it. The sensation cannot be forced or manipulated like an orgasm purely of the sexual physical body, and rather than beginning from the bottom and working its way up, this ecstasy, originating within the energy body, begins from the top, opens and melts downward. Is that a good description of what you felt?" she asked.

"It's close to perfection," I responded with awe.

"Have you ever had such a sensation before?"

"Sometimes, during the climax of a beautiful piece of music, or a magnificent soliloquy. At times, tears will involuntarily wash over my eyes as well," I said. For some reason my voice was trembling, as though I were about to cry.

"It means you are very sensitive and powerfully passionate," she said softly. "What you experienced is the energy body's orgasm. It cannot be manufactured. Sometimes it can be cultivated by teaching others to be more sensitive, but many live a lifetime without ever feeling what you just felt, even once."

"Perhaps I know what you mean," I said. "I saw a film once about the composer Mozart and a contemporary, the composer Salieri, who despite all his efforts could never once feel or hear the inspiration from which sprang Mozart's compositions. Salieri was moved to heights by the music, but he wanted to create such bliss himself. He was never able, and even asked Mozart to explain his inspiration, which still did not change Salieri's ability."

"You are also very artistic," doña Celestina replied. "Had you been born full-blooded, into a Native community, no doubt you would have been a peerless weaver or basket maker. Your story focuses in on exactly what I was trying to explain. The sensation happens by grace. It is a blessing that is spontaneous. It cannot be forced, or taught, or copied. You are a very lucky woman. Yes, you weave very well, Merlina.

"Perhaps you should weave with words," she pondered thoughtfully, "one of the tools of your culture. Become a storyteller. Storytellers are highly respected artists among Native people. Many were and are women. You have a gift. In our culture, though, the storytellers never wrote down their stories, so you would be an exception. I think that you are always the exception to the rule, Merlina." She nodded silently to herself.

"That's very kind of you to say, doña," I replied. "I have certainly seen, heard, and learned more than enough from all of you to spin some very good tales."

"I don't flatter," she asserted. "If I see the energy, I call it by its right name, that's all. Inspiration, as you call it, or ecstasy, is one of the highly evolved manifestations of sexual energy, but not the sexual energy of the physical body alone. Rather, we are moving now into expressions of the evolving sexual energy of the energy body. The sensation you felt can also occur during powerful expressions of Dreaming. It is as though the luminous butterfly begins to emerge from its luminous cocoon and experiences the thrill of being what it is truly becoming. That takes energy, Merlina, and a tremendous amount of work. You are there. Again I repeat that you are truly fortunate.

"Some people never get to this place on the path, despite a lifetime of efforts they remain terrestrial. What this means is that you are going to be with us now even longer than you expected. Don Juan, Chon, and I will have some additional gems to share with you, even beyond what we had already planned, some of the crowning stones of the path. Congratulations. You've earned it."

I didn't quite know what to say. "Perhaps this experience might be easier for some to seek in Dreaming, away from the daily grind and the lack of inspiration due to our consensus agreement of ordinary perceptions?" I suggested.

"It won't happen if the individual is not ready to be moved," she said. "If their islands are not swept clean, people sabotage themselves with trivia. And then there is the matter of being blessed on the inside. One must cultivate a free-floating, genuine, magical nature, not an easy thing to do in this world. Such a nature is as rare as the magical deer of the Bacatete Sierra among the Yaqui, south of here."

"Still, if one Dreams with this intent and sets it up as a task, what does one do?" I asked.

"One might begin by Dreaming one's evolving sexual energy," she replied. "In that way, the Dreamer would be within the domain proper of the energy body, providing that the individual is lucid, awakened within the Dream, and visionary, and not indulging in nonawakened, base symbolic dreams dealing with urges, repressions and the like."

"I see." (Doña Celestina sets up tasks with the consummate artistry of her superlative beadwork, I thought to myself. There is much to learn in their design.)

"They might not like what they see, but it would be a start, providing they can Dream," she went on. "Then again, there are occasional pleasant surprises. At the very least, it would activate the process of sensitization, of seeing the sexual energies as energetically evolutionary, rather than merely procreative. Such a task would foster creativity, and could lead to inspiration, giving them a glimpse of directions in which they might like to move. The energy body is devoid of ego, you see, so if these practices are undertaken in Dreaming, again providing that one is truly awakened within the Dream, the energy body will show a truthful view. That would be an advantage. Most people have a great deal of ego and competitiveness surrounding their sexual energy while they conceive of themselves only as expressions of a physical body. I wonder, though, why do you ask all these questions? Are you thinking of teaching people how to Dream?"

"Chon has suggested it," I volunteered.

"That would be interesting," she mused. "It could only be of benefit, as long as you are careful what you show them; nothing of the dastardly deeds I sometimes have to do or undo. Why don't you go back to bed now and try the task I shared with you? Never ask anyone to do something you haven't navigated yourself first, if you are truly interested in accepting such a responsibility."

I thanked her and got up and returned to my room. It would now be quite easy to fall asleep. The wind was silent, and the soft rain a mere mist. The night was still and soothing and I was very, very sleepy. The last thing I heard before entering Dreaming was the call of a quail that had perhaps alighted and perched on a branch of her papaya tree.

With the intent of my task behind the force of my lucidity, I awakened into the realization that I was Dreaming when I found myself surrounded by a golden-white light emptiness. There was a soft tone resonating which reminded me of the sound of a crystal bowl softly ringing. The sound permeated the light. In fact, it was the light and the light was the sound. This was my energy, unconfigured, as don Juan had explained, expressing nothing but my luminous nature and my awareness.

The Dreaming followed me into the first moments of opening my eyes at early morning. I found the air to be animated, filled with globules of luminous matter that I was able to catch with my fingertips and direct into a spin around one another, like atoms or tiny solar systems. I kept closing my eyes, expecting the effect to go away, but it didn't. Each time I opened my eyes again, there was the luminous scene, the globules and the possibility of putting them in little groups to spin around one another. The texture of the substance felt like pure creative energy and I sensed myself as the essence of creativity.

Finally, after several consecutive experiences, I felt as though a part of me went very lightly to sleep and I found myself in my normal state of awareness, but left with the afterglow. I realized at that moment what Chon has always professed to me about Dreaming, that in our normal state of awareness we are actually more asleep than when we Dream.

PRACTICE FIFTEEN

DREAMING THE EVOLVING SEXUAL ENERGY

1. The Dreaming intent is to See the evolutionary process of your sexual energies. Set up this intent as your task. Each night upon retiring, repeat the task to yourself over and over again, either mentally or with spoken words, as you enter sleep.

2. During Dreaming, intend nothing but the view of your own sexual energies, as though you were trying to see the formation of a butterfly within a translucent chrysalis. Disturb nothing.

3. The view will be different for each individual. Once, I Saw my own energy as a long series of rounded humps, which at first appeared to be an endless expanse of ancient green hills. Later, when they moved, I realized the energy to be more like the rippling body of a massive water serpent. On another occasion, my sexual energy rose, greenish-golden and phoenixlike, from a pool of burning embers.

4. This task speaks directly to the energy body, and so in that sense it is not a difficult intent to set up. However, it does require Dreaming energy, and without a sufficient quantity in reserve it cannot easily be accomplished.

5. The best avenues for storing Dreaming energy are all of the fire breath practices, drawing and releasing energy in nature, thorough recapitulation and energy retrieval, and the wise conservation of sexual energies.

THE PHALLIC
FEMALE

IN THE MID-MORNING, AFTER BATHING AND DRESSING, I found doña Celestina waiting for me on the patio, holding a cup of hot chocolate. Her mood was both enthusiastic and severe as she handed me the steaming mug and motioned for me to follow her into the altar room.

"The nagual Juan has asked us to accelerate our pace with you, based on what he Saw of your maneuvers in Dreaming last night," she said as we walked through the passageway. "Today our topic will be phallic energy. We will look at its presence in both males and females."

I eagerly anticipated the discussion. Upon entering her workroom I found that she had again pulled the curtains back, allowing the sunlight to illuminate every well-dusted surface. The room veritably glowed with the warmth of morning light. The furniture seemed to be curiously alive and humming, although I could not account for the perception.

"You're right. All energy is alive," she noted, as if sensing my thoughts.

Her altar table was cleared of implements, with the exception of a very long, clear, crystal wand, shimmering as it was touched by a ray of light. I was drawn to the crystal, noticing that the surface was covered by naturally occurring geometric designs, thinly etched by its formation into the hardness of its luminous clarity. Its length was greater than that of my hand, and its diameter, approximately as big around as my second finger.

"The nagual found that for you in the Kofa Mountains, northeast of Yuma," doña Celestina told me, urging me with her eyes to take an even closer look.

"This is mine?" I asked with astonishment, transfixed by the radiant crystal.

"Yes. Have a seat at the table, Merlina. You see," she said as she seated herself and pointed at the length of crystal, "this is the phallic energy within the central internal energy column. Actually, there are three internal columns within the body that carry energy. The one in the back is masculine, the column in the front is feminine and the central column is balanced. It is both male and female, well . . . a hermaphrodite."

I pulled my seat closer.

"Not everyone has one of these inside their bodies. Naturally, all men think they do," she laughed, "but many do not, and many women no longer have this energy within them. The base of the crystalline column starts at the root of the genitals. It remains semierect all of the time, and when aroused, it can rise far above the height of the head. Questions?"

"Yes. How is it lost, or rather, why is it given to some and not to others? Can this energy be gained or reclaimed? And, what arouses the energy, what constitutes its arousal?" I was keen with interest.

"Those are very good questions," she said approvingly, nodding her head. "First, for a child to be born with this energy in the body, both its mother and father must have had it, since the central column is a balance of masculine and feminine. Also, the parents must have been powerful, in order to provide the necessary force. If the woman lent her phallic energy to the man, if she denied herself and allowed her energy to be brutalized, then she would not have been able to make the necessary contribution at conception, which must, by the way, be accompanied by a powerful orgasm. Without the dynamic of orgasm, the conception would lack force.

"The male partner, on the other hand, must have received the energy from both his mother and father. If his mother was lacking, or if his father's mother was lacking, and so on, he would not inherit. It really does begin and end with the female. The female and male infants must inherit from energetically complete parents. That is the only way to be born complete. Again, I say that if the mother or the father have lost the balanced phallic energy on either side of their family, the offspring will not be born with a full dose. This can go back for generations.

"In order to gain or reclaim the energy, as you put it, one must retrace the steps and recapitulate the memory of one's conception and the parents" and grandparents" contributions. In doing this recapitulation, naturally, one must be in an isolated place for a very long time, away from all sensory stimuli, and be in a mode of pure, powerful, and far-reaching introspection. One will sense the vacuity, the giveaway, if you will, as a hollow, flaccid feeling within one's own energetic makeup while reflecting upon the individual who initiated the hereditary depletion. That is where one seeks to effect change, beginning there and then retracing forward again in time.

"One must stalk the responsible party or parties. If they are dead, that means journeying into other realms where vestiges of their energy may still remain. There, one may seek to undo what was done and rightfully claim the energy one is able to retrieve. By virtue of being heir to the energy, one will be naturally imbued after taking the corrective measures.

"The challenge may come in the form of a quest. For example, by Dreaming Awake, as you know, one may open gateways into other realms and enter with the body intact, in order to do battle. I say as you know, because you have done this with Juan and Chon on many necessary occasions. You actually stepped across a lake of energy into another realm on one occasion, and could have even remained there, had you chosen to do so. Your battle, however, was elsewhere."

The experience to which she referred was the subject of a chapter in my first book. It was a battle of life and death for me. She was correct. I had, in fact, on many occasions walked across a bridge into other realms Dreaming Awake, opening a vortex, separating a veil of energy if you will, using the practice. Don Juan maintained that this practice entails entering realms usually reserved for the death and after-death states. As such it has to be regarded seriously by shamans, sorcerers, and healers, since it produces a "little death" for the practitioner. I could easily envision the battles of power, life, and death, that would ensue. Don Juan had often told me that one only enters these realms in order to look for that which has been lost, be it power, health, or clarity of purpose and vision. He said that great temptation and illusion lie within these realms and that many a practitioner has become too heavy laden to leave, having lost all sense of sobriety.

"You can see," doña Celestina went on in a measured tone, "that, due to the daunting task of the energy's retrieval, most people just won't bother. Not being prepared to make the journey, perhaps they are wise. However, the energy is necessary. A healer like Chon, perhaps, can go in and undertake part of the battle for an individual in life-or-death circumstances, but remember that, ultimately, the one who does the work receives the largest blessing.

"Assuming that the energy is in place within the body, this opens up all of the possibilities in the true intent of creation itself, and it is this creative principal which when understood or experienced, will arouse and awaken the energy. When aroused, it arises like a crystalline shaft through the central column and reaches untold heights. The shaft of light hums. It sings. It knows. It resonates with purity, pure truth, pure love, pure beauty, strength, wisdom . . . and it tempers itself with work and humility.

"Only someone who is in possession of this internal force will move on to the most advanced revelations on the path. Many of these involve death and after-death transformations. This is where the nagual wants us to take you. He will leave very soon, you see, and he wants us to prepare you because he is going to take you part of the way."

She picked up the crystal and handed it to me. Placing it between my palms, I could feel a vibration within it. Doña Celestina rose and went to one of her cabinets. After searching briefly, she brought out a small tubular chime. Asking me to hold the crystal shaft up to my ear, she struck the chime. The vibration registered within the crystal, which resonated sympathetically at a softer, lower pitch. The tone was beautiful and long lived. I was quite stilled by it. Yet I had burning questions.

"I'm very concerned by what you have just told me of don Juan's impending departure, doña Celestina," I said, taking the opportunity to voice my feelings. "I suspect, based upon what you have both been telling me, that you are referring to his imminent departure from being human, that he is preparing somehow to leave this world as we know it."

"As some know it," she replied, "but not as you and I will know it, and not as Chon knows it. You are right. You needn't worry. We are going to prepare you thoroughly. He will not leave the world the way most do, not the way Carlo Castillo is going to leave, for example. And he will not go where most disintegrate. That is what he is going to prepare you for."

She shocked me by bringing up Carlo Castillo's impending death from cancer. I could tell by having seen him that there was no way he was going to beat it. There had always been a bit of bad blood between Carlo and doña Celestina, and yet what I heard from her was not vengeance. It was just the simple voice of truth. I surmised that most who knew Carlo, including Carlo himself, were totally unprepared for his death, which was inevitable. That was not the case for doña Celestina. She, like I, saw the situation clearly and refused not to call a spade a spade.

Sensing my reflections, she moved closer to me and looked me in the eyes, nodding gently. "The old nagual is going to walk out of this world," doña Celestina told me plainly, and that is all that she would say about it for the moment.

PRACTICE SIXTEEN

DREAMING AWAKE

1. This practice is an application of Dream Bridging (see page 11), yet it is much more expansive. Rather than selecting an item, or a person, or even an ordinary place as the focus of your intent in Dreaming and the bridge into the waking realm, select an opening into awakened Dreaming as the object of intent.

2. For example, you Dream that you enter your garden at night by the light of the moon. You awaken fully within the Dream to realize that you are actually present there as your energy double. Then you add the next touch. You Dream that any time you enter your garden at night with such a moonlight, you will be able to access your double energy. This is adding strategy. You Dream that on any such occasion, when you are present in that garden it will be as your energy double, just as it is now.

3. This opens some of the possibilities of bringing the double fully into the waking world, through a specially designed gateway, your garden in the moonlight. Once a gateway is bridged into the waking world, it will remain until it has served its intended purpose. This purpose is selected by power itself, and not by the petty designs of the ego. A gateway is different from a bridge in that a gateway is an opening, while a bridge is merely a means to cross back and forth.

4. It is through such a Dreamed and bridged gateway that one may later travel into other realms, or forward or backward in time, with the physical body intact. Think of such a gateway as a wormhole in the fabric of the Dream of space and time, for that is its true nature. Think of a bridge as a foundation you lay in order to build a gateway.

LIFE-FORCE
ENERGY DANCE

I LEFT DOÑA CELESTINA'S ALTAR ROOM LATER IN THE DAY IN order to have lunch, which Chencha informed us could be served whenever we wished. As I walked through the dark passage and reached the archways, I found Chon dancing around the patio, completely oblivious to any potential audience. The music playing was lively and his movements swept to and fro in the most curious manner I had ever seen.

I paused for a moment to take him in. He smiled at me, now aware of my presence, and then returned his concentration to the dance. Hopping about, gesticulating here and there, his movements were at times wildly sharp and then suddenly graceful, attaining the smoothness of a feather's fall.

"Looks like fun," I said, grinning, not knowing what to make of him.

When the song was over, he walked a short distance to turn off the new portable radio/cassette player I had purchased in San Luis, and motioned for me to join him on the patio. "This is quite a contraption," he commented with approval. "It produces a lot of noise for its small size!"

"What were you up to?" I teased. "What kind of dancing was that?"

He grinned. "Oh, that wasn't dancing, not really," he said,

raising his arched brows. "That was today's conversation with energy."

"Really?" I played along. "Is that what you call what you were doing?"

Chon laughed. "Want to try it?" he invited me.

That caught me rather off guard. "I suppose so," I replied. "Just exactly how do I do it?"

"Well," he said with a smirk, "let's talk to serpent! Go back to the energy of Dreaming serpent. Just bridge that intent right here onto this patio, Merlina. Let that energy move your physical body and energy will become your teacher. That is as it should be. People come and go but energy endures, never created or destroyed. Energy simply is, yet it changes forms. Try it!" His eyes invited me to accept his proposition and attempt the task.

Surprisingly, it was not at all difficult to shift my awareness into the Dream of serpent which I had experienced with don Juan in the canyon, days before. The golden serpent energy was already vibrantly present and awakened within me. All I had to do was silence my mind and intend the awareness. Chon sensed this readily.

"Shifting into Dreaming energy is becoming easier for you. Now roll your eyes up and back into your head," he guided me. "Try to look inside of your head at the single point between your eyebrows," Chon touched the corresponding spot on my forehead with his index finger.

The moment he did so, I heard a humming. It was exactly the same tone I had experienced the night before, Dreaming my sexual energies under doña Celestina's guidance. I focused my inner gaze upon the precise spot.

"Allow the energy to move inside of you," Chon said to me. "It will work its way through any blocks there may be and will then begin to talk to your body, guiding it of its own accord, in the ways that it should move in order to express the energy flowing through it." He slapped me on the back between the shoulders and urged me to let go.

The first sensation was one of heat. As I connected inwardly with the energy, it was as though the flame of a blow torch had been ignited. Within me, all obstacles in its path were reduced to ash. My face and body flushed and I perspired profusely. And then, just as quickly, the blast turned into a dry heat. I felt my skin tingle and become excited, effervescent and firm. A sense of exhilaration thrilled my being and I was as light as the breeze, filled with boundless energy.

"Let the energy express itself to you through movement," Chon said to me.

All at once, my arms rose above my head, elongated and drifted, swaying like flames in the breeze. My spine began to ripple until my whole body was the dancing flame, alive with a glowing energy which I could perceive physically and within my peripheral vision. Somehow, I was burning without being consumed. As the heat began to rise further within me, it created a sensation of lightheadedness. At one moment my arms extended, outstretched across the horizontal plane, and undulated like serpents.

"Eagle eats serpent. Serpent becomes eagle," Chon remarked cryptically.

My body responded before my mind could process his words. In one instant the motion of my arms was transformed into a soaring, gliding, elevating beat in unison. Then my body, overtaken by the sweep of wings, began to circle and Chon joined in with his magical birdlike hopping.

Suddenly I felt a wriggling inside of me, as if some unknown energy was now trying to emerge from a cocoon that was my body and, before I understood what was happening, I had altered my movements again and was dancing "moth." Chon's body seemed instantly to understand my message in movement. He responded with moth movements of awesome power, spontaneity, and grace. I was struck with the impression that never in my life had I experienced a more profound symbiotic communication.

Chon went over to the radio and turned the music on again. A piercing Veracruzana began and he commenced with a frolicking stomp, which I improvised until I was giddy beyond words and hyperventilating with laughter.

At the next song, don Juan emerged out of the dark passageway, dressed in the solid black he often wore, having just returned from a long walk. Somehow the entire afternoon had passed by without my noticing, and twilight was approaching. I became disoriented, and the music seemed to insist upon my attention. I could swear that I had the feeling of time speeding up, and yet I had no way to account for this perception.

The following tune was a "chicken scratch," like a wildly twirling Mexican polka but without words, highly popular at Yaqui and Papago festivities of the region. Before I knew it, don Juan grabbed me and we were off. A master of the two-step, a modern version of what Native Americans call "bird dancing," he had me spinning within a heartbeat, semicircles, circles, and then full-tilt whirls around the patio. He only let go of me when my head began pounding and my heart racing so that I could not draw my breath.

I held on to one of the rocking chairs until my composure returned to me and my chest ceased to heave. Don Juan winked at me and gave Chon an eye signal as he left the patio, which evidently meant "turn off the music." I collapsed into a chair and Chon pulled up another beside me. He sat and relaxed with great pleasure, lighthearted, and with a huge smile across his face.

"You can get high from dancing," he told me and laughed.

"I'm curious, Chon," I asked him, once I had my breath back. "Do your healing movements originate in Dreaming as well?"

"Do you mean like my dancing?" he asked laughing, extending the word "dancing" to ridiculous lengths, opening his eyes as wide as possible.

"Let me put it this way, Chon. All of your moves seem quite original." I told him.

"As you have seen, anyone can do it!" he replied, smiling. "All that is necessary is to Dream energy to the body for a specific purpose and then bridge that energy into the waking world. My specific purpose for this afternoon was sheer pleasure."

"Can you give me some examples of Dreaming energy to the body?" I asked him.

"Sure!" he exclaimed. "I'm filled with them! For example. . ." he began, using an exaggeratedly pedantic tone, "let's say that you want to feed an area of your body with extra energy to be used for an extraordinary healing, for either yourself, someone else or even for both, since there is no reason that a healer should become depleted. You begin by intending energy to that area in Dreaming. Or perhaps intend the energy to your hands, which will later be placed near the area in question. Next, refine the energy in Dreaming. Work with it until it becomes exquisite, exact, and effective. Dream it over and over again. Then bridge the energy into the waking world by performing whatever support tasks you may be shown in Dreaming that accompany the energy.

"I often see some kind of movement associated with the energy in its most refined expression. That movement is usually very slight and concentrated, and consequently very easy to bridge. This signals me that the energy is now efficient, educated if you will, and ready to be used. That's when I bridge it, by performing the signals or support movements. Sometimes, instead of a movement, I generate a feeling from Dreaming in order to call the energy. This is also very effective, especially if I direct the feeling towards the specific area in question with my intent.

"An important point is always to perfect the energy by Dreaming and re-Dreaming it, before actually applying it in the waking world. This process can be undertaken for the sheer joy of it! One may even Dream a dance that generates well-being, freedom of spirit and power. We must always remember to play! It keeps us from becoming too heavy."

"This process seems as though it could be very effective for self-healing, as well as for developing healers," I interjected.

"Absolutely," Chon agreed. "It even has applications beyond the scope of healing. Using these practices, with the appropriate intent, of course, one may actually collect, concentrate, and refine the ultimate wealth, life force, and purified awareness, and pack them into both the physical and the energy body. Many people focus all of their dreams of a good life on material possessions, entertaining experiences, romance, control, or professional success. They forget entirely about investing their Dreams in their own life force, and in their own transformations at death. When their number is called, they come up extremely short in that department, I can tell you.

"Most people are totally unprepared for their last moments on Earth. They waste their sexual and vital energies on baubles that cannot be cashed in at Death. They die the way they do because they have run out of life. Juan wants us to speak with you about ultimate experiences, and show you where practitioners store their treasures and how they cash them in. You are going to have some intense lessons now, Merlina, and you may see true marvels. Knowing how to store energy in your body by using Dreaming is only the beginning."

Chon then stood up and reached toward the sky as if drawing energy directly from it. He made semicircular movements with his hands and slowly brought them down to the level of his internal organs. He stroked his sides and said "Collect, concentrate, purify, and pack."

PRACTICE SEVENTEEN

DREAMING ENERGY INTO THE BODY
WITH MAGICAL MOVEMENTS

1. Focus your Dreaming intent upon the area of your body that you wish to energize. Selecting vital areas such as internal organs or bones is best, unless you have disease in a specific area that you wish to focus upon.
2. Intend in Dreaming that energy will come to this area in a perceivable manner and allow the process to occur, maintaining your lucidity.
3. Focus now upon refining the frequency by enhancing such qualities as purity, light, ecstatic wave, and amplitude. Use the force of your intent to guide and modulate the energy.
4. Fine-tune the energy into the specifically desired area, directing its level of penetration with the force of your intent.
5. Concentrate all of these acts into one "cue," a gesture coupled with a powerful intent, which may be bridged into the waking world. Practice these steps in Dreaming until the process is smooth and effortless.
6. Bridge the energy by maintaining the Dreamed intent while performing the "cue" in the waking world, in the manner in which it was Dreamed.

SACRED
UNION

I WALKED OUT ONTO THE PATIO THE NEXT MORNING AND found it freshly decorated with vases of fragrant white roses and gardenias. No one was about. I knew the gardenias must have been sent from a moister climate and I couldn't imagine who might have brought them. I paused to take in the mild, autumn sunlight and early morning desert breeze. The patio was absolutely immaculate, glistening and solitary. Deciding to linger in the light near the blissful fragrance of the gardenias, I poured myself a cool glass of tamarind lemonade in the kitchen and returned to the patio to sit down in a rocking chair and read.

I must have dozed off, because my next memory is of opening my eyes to find that it was about 10 o'clock in the morning. Don Juan was standing at the foot of my chair in his khakis and hat, peering into my face. For a moment, as my eyes adjusted to the brighter morning light, I was unable to distinguish between his smiling face and the rising sun immediately behind him.

"Let's go across the border to the Gila River today," he suggested.

It was a wonderful idea. I smiled dreamily and got my car keys without a word. We went out back and got into the jeep, accompanied by the same blissful silence and peace. When we arrived at the border checkpoint, the American agent didn't pay any attention at all to the old Indian in the passenger seat. He merely looked into my still-dreaming eyes and asked, "What was the purpose of your visit to Mexico, ma'am?"

"Oh, I was just shopping," I replied casually.

"Go ahead, ma'am, and have a nice day." The agent nodded and waved me on through the checkpoint as don Juan sighed and reclined with satisfaction in the front seat, pulling his hat down over his face to hide a smile.

We drove for a while, east beyond Yuma, until we reached the open desert of the Gila River which travels southwest and eventually merges with the Colorado. Stepping out of the parked jeep alongside the banks, I immediately sensed the spirit of the Gila to be quite different from that of the Colorado. While the Colorado River has a forceful spirit, even though it has been slowed by dams and has dwindled due to irrigation, the Gila seems more playful. At this point along the river the water was flowing rapidly, unhindered by man-made trappings. Surrounded by bald blue lava mountains to the east and west, the area was a perfect place for our conversation.

I pulled two straw mats out of the back and handed them to don Juan, so that he might set them near the river in a comfortable spot. I also brought out a gourd of water and some of the locally dried dates. Placing my hat upon my head, I joined him under the mesquite he had selected. The view from that spot was spectacular. Seated along the southerly bank, with a large saguaro field to our north, we could hear the flow of the Gila in front of us, which sounded like the giggling of a small child, and observe the drift of occasional white clouds and the flight of birds.

No sooner than I was seated an elf owl peeked his tiny head out of a hole at the very top of a large saguaro cactus. The area abounded with jack rabbits, roadrunners, and hawks, all of which darted about on their morning errands.

"Everyone enjoys the river," don Juan chuckled as we watched the wildlife scurrying and adjusting to our presence. "I thought today might be the perfect day to talk with you about love," he said, taking a large medjul date and savoring a bite of the golden brown flesh.

I peered at his twinkling eyes underneath the shadow cast by the brim of his hat. "I was hoping we wouldn't leave it out," I said, smiling. "No more stories of Melquior Ángelo, I hope."

He laughed and slapped his thigh. "Nope. Your point is well taken. Many teachers and practitioners get so caught up in the acquisition of new powers that they seemingly forget all about love. Yet when and if they are ever fortunate enough for the real thing to present itself in front of their faces, well, I assure you, they are caught just as unprepared as anyone else. I thought I might bring you here and tell you the story of the magical deer in order to illustrate my point."

I settled back on the mat so that I might listen to don Juan with full awareness. Don Juan's mastery of Native storytelling was peerless, and his timing and setting were impeccable.

"It seems there was a young sorcerer's apprentice," he began, "who lived in this desert, abounding with wildlife." He extended his arm in a sweeping gesture all around the horizon. "He wished for the power of abundance in order that he might become a wealthy and renowned man, able to attract any girl he might so choose. He came out to this area here on a vision quest for the power and spent night after night in an isolated spot, without food or water, supplicating to the forces and spirits that dwell here, crying out his desire and his intent.

"The first creature to approach him was mountain lion. On the first night of his quest the she cat offered him force and cunning, but this was not what he sought. He said thank you but would not accept the offer. The next night as he sat within a circle crying to the forces, coyote appeared, offering him sly fearlessness and charisma. The young fellow thought about it, swayed somewhat by coyote's deceptive charm, but in the end he said no thank you, and coyote went on. On the third night owl appeared and spoke to him, saying, 'I can offer you seeing, for I assure you that you do not know what it is that you want. You lack discernment.' The young apprentice was stubbornly set in his desire, however, and would not accept.

"On the fourth night the young apprentice was beside himself with hunger and thirst, but still stubborn in his resolve. As he lay half-delirious within the circle, a vision appeared. There, in front of his eyes, a magical deer shimmered before him. He could tell right off that this was no ordinary creature. It moved with a grace never before seen, and its luminosity . . ." don Juan paused a moment for dramatic effect.

"Yet there was something elusive about the creature," he continued, "as if its powers could not be possessed. Still it stood there, fully tangible. That made the young apprentice want the beautiful apparition all the more.

"She spoke to him in a liquid female voice. 'I have heard your cries and have taken pity on you,' she told him. 'I can give you a taste of that power you seek, that which is most valuable in creation, but once you have tried it nothing else will compare to it and you will be fated to seek it always and everywhere.'

"The young man salivated with the thought of the most valuable power. Surely, through it he would become the wealthiest and most powerful among men. 'I accept,' he said without hesitation. The magical deer nodded and suddenly the young man saw that she was transforming into something so beautiful, so inconceivable, that even his eyes were overtaken with the inability to express it. He felt touched down to the very core of his being and began to weep, covering his face in shame.

"'Why do you hide your eyes from that which you wish?' she asked him. Even her voice was transformed. 'Is this not what you want?' So he uncovered his face and looked upon a creature, the likes of which he had never seen. He felt such a love, a love that he could not explain, a love almost beyond the bounds of the desire for the power he sought. Surely, the gift of this being was going to be miraculous. And then, she vanished."

"What?" I said, raising up to prop myself on my elbows.

"She left him," don Juan repeated.

There was silence. Even the river was hushed for a moment. I thought about his tale, pondering in the silence and in the breeze all that he had said to me. "So her gift was transformation," I said.

"And the love that he felt," don Juan added.

"Did he ever see her again?" I asked him.

"One would hope so," he replied. "We cannot know that. All we can know is that he searched for her always and everywhere, even to the end of his life, even beyond death."

There was a passion in don Juan's voice that had brought tears to my eyes and caused my throat to clench. I was trembling and on the verge of full-blown sobs. "Have you ever known a feeling like that?" I asked him.

"I have," he replied, looking fully into my eyes.

I grasped the ground as I felt my breath leap out of me.

"You needn't worry," he said.

But I *was* worried, and I didn't know why. I felt so agitated that I thought I might explode into molecules and particles at any moment. Don Juan took off his hat, smoothed his hair and turned my face toward his, putting his finger under my chin. He looked at me for a long moment, looking so calmly into my eyes, and then gently leaned forward, touching the crown of his forehead with my own.

In that moment I felt the most incredible, indescribable feeling of peace and love, beyond anything I have ever felt. Everything vanished and, beneath my closed lids, we and all around us were one, and filled with golden white light.

PRACTICE EIGHTEEN

MERGING MEDITATION

1. This is a beautiful practice used by shifters, to become one with the object of their intent. It may be used by lovers or friends also, to become one with one another.

2. Begin by being seated at arm's length, directly across from one another. Empty the mind of all thoughts and breathe from the belly, expanding the abdomen in a relaxed manner on the inhale.

3. Gaze profoundly and with a silent mind into one another's eyes. Allow yourself to be filled with the other, completely emptying of your self. Don't judge, fear, or cling in any way.

4. At a given moment, make room for the other within you. Do this by gently extending your right arm forward. This says to the other energetically "I make room for you within me."

5. Gently retract the arm and place it at your side. This says energetically to your partner "I make room for me within you."

6. The partner responds by doing the same movements at the appropriate moment. Note: This practice will often bring up overwhelming feelings and the eyes may fill with tears. The tears cleanse the window of the eyes. Do not allow yourself to break down and indulge in sobs. In order to hold energy, the vessel must not be cracked. Simply stay with the flood of feelings and breathe. Gaze through the tears.

7. The effect of this practice is so profound that it may synchronize your brain waves. You may notice minor telltale signs afterwards, such as slight identical movements shared between you, perhaps even performed at the same moment.

THE
UNICORN

CHON AND DOÑA CELESTINA CAME INTO THE kitchen the following morning while I was helping myself to *huevos rancheros,* free-range eggs served on freshly-made corn tortillas, smothered in green chili and tomatillo sauce. Chon poured himself a cup of hot coffee and sat down with me at the table. Doña Celestina inspected my cooking approvingly, prepared two eggs for herself and then joined us. I was surprised to encounter both of them together, especially since they each had a mood of expectation, signaling me that I was to give them my undivided attention after breakfast.

"We want to talk with you about the four energetic compartments of a balanced energy being," Chon began, sensing my curiosity. "Don't worry. We're not going to fight over you." He giggled and gave doña Celestina a wink, having put words to my unspoken thoughts. "Actually, it will take all three of us to explain them properly to you, so Juan will be joining us later. For now, enjoy your breakfast and when you feel that the time is right, come out to the little healing room that I have set up in the back."

I nodded my assent and continued with my meal. Chon took his coffee and walked out onto the patio. Doña Celestina remained with me at the table and ate her breakfast in silence. I could tell by the expression in her eyes that she was extremely pleased by something. Their bright, mischievous twinkle was the only indication, however, in her otherwise forceful presence. I never ceased to marvel at the sheer strength of her.

After washing the dishes and tidying up the kitchen, I walked back to my room and spent some time writing in my journal. Writing helped me not only to consolidate their lessons, but also to empty myself of the feelings associated with them so that I could be clear for the next step of the new work, whatever that might be. Doña Celestina reminded me continually that a woman is at her most powerful when she is silent and empty, and don Juan often added that it is this same state that lends a warrior the necessary sobriety and dispassion to come through and to fulfill effectively whatever tasks fate may place along the path. With these thoughts in mind, when the time was right I walked back to the healing room where all three of them were waiting for me.

When I peered into the door of the room, I saw that it was furnished only with four straight-backed chairs, three of which were occupied. Everyone rose to greet me.

"Let's get to work!" don Juan said enthusiastically.

They clustered around me and each person in turn slapped me between the shoulder blades at a different spot on my back. Don Juan pulled my chair towards me so that I might be seated and they each seated themselves. Everyone held my gaze and then Chon began to speak.

"It should be no surprise to you that each of us has put a portion of our own energy into you," Chon said, looking at me directly. "You've had three teachers and three benefactors and each of us has addressed a different area of your energy body, assigning you tasks and filling you with knowledge proper to the respective domains. Our intent has been to create stability in you, and we feel that we've succeeded."

Doña Celestina continued. "A powerful structure must be balanced or it will topple over. Four is the number of stability and four is the number of energetic compartments within a fully actualized energy being."

Don Juan spoke next. "Every human being is born with the capacity for four energetic compartments, but few individuals realize their activation. In order to journey the length of this path, all four compartments must be operative and must receive the knowledge proper to each."

At this point they all waited to see if I had questions. I felt that I had none, and so they proceeded further. "You might say that each of us, or rather the knowledge we have imparted to you, pertains to a different energetic compartment," doña Celestina said.

"We have actually put points of knowledge and awareness within you that we have assembled ourselves, or have assembled with the help of our own teachers," Chon added. "In that sense, there is great continuity to what we have done."

Don Juan then asked me to open my palm. I did so and he drew a small sign upon it with the tip of his index finger. The symbol was rather like a four-petaled flower, with another, identical to the first, superimposed upon it. A small round opening was centrally located within them both. "These are the four compartments of the physical body," he said, tapping the first four petals. "The next four are the compartments of the energy body. When fully developed, they are identical to the first four and yet more evolved. The opening is into the creation void," he said. "This is the configuration of an actualized human being."

Everything they were saying seemed perfectly clear to me. I could see how each of them was an archetype of one of the four compartments, and also how each of my mentors had the four compartments operating within them. I nodded my understanding and they went on.

"In order for the energy body to be able to accelerate properly at the moment of death, in order for it to be able to spin on balance and not lose momentum, in order for the energy not to topple or gyrate in an undesirable direction or 'go cold,' the four petals need not only to be activated, but also to be developed in a balanced manner, each compartment able to wield more or less the same amount of force, each able to work with the others, and each approximately the same size. If you visualize a broken propeller, you will easily see what I mean," Chon told me.

I adjusted my awareness, for the lesson had now taken on quite a serious and final kind of tone. I focused upon listening fully in silence.

"We feel that you are balanced and, when the time comes, you will be able to move into realms of energy that are not of this Earth," doña Celestina said.

That comment jolted me.

"Juan is ready and so he is going to take you with him part of the way, if you agree," Chon stated plainly, staring into my eyes.

Now I was flooded with thoughts and perceptions, queries, emotions, and even fears.

I looked at don Juan, who raised his brows slightly as if to reiterate Chon's question.

"Just as we have given you a piece of ourselves, so have we also taken a piece of you. It is as simple as that," don Juan said to me. "We will always be connected and yet we are free. It is an even trade."

"Because of this," Chon went on, "wherever we journey,

the others may learn and prepare. Someone is always preparing the way, because a portion of each of us is with the other. Do you agree to this?"

Something other than my normal daily awareness heard every word spoken to me and answered the query clearly, simply, and with sober intent. "I do," I said.

With that, a force was forged. They asked me to rise from my seat and each of them did so in turn. Doña Celestina stood to my right front, don Juan to my right back, Chon to my left back and nothingness to my left front.

"This is the configuration," doña Celestina said. "In this way we are balanced warriors. To your front is water, to your back, fire. To the right of you, your masculine, to the left, your feminine. To the right is force, to the left is suppleness. To the right is power and action, to the left, silence and emptiness. In the center is your longevity and your balance, your wisdom and your way." She touched the identical place at the crown of my forehead that don Juan had touched with his own, the day before. The tip of her right index finger rested there and then spiraled gracefully in a counterclockwise direction.

Then she, don Juan, and Chon all simultaneously clapped their hands once loudly, as if to catch some ineffable something flying through the air, and I felt as though I had awakened from a Dream. Don Juan patted me gently on the back.

"Let's go get some lemonade," he suggested. "We can talk a little more after a few moments."

A bit of a break did me quite a lot of good. Chon and doña Celestina went about their business while don Juan and I enjoyed tall glasses of hibiscus lemonade on the patio. This day was just as beautiful as the one before had been. The temperature was now becoming springlike every day, with cloudless or near cloudless skies and a mild breeze, and the climate would remain so until April, when the temperatures would again begin to rise towards their fiery climax in the months of July and August.

I relaxed and put my head back against the rocking chair. This was the first time my body had really registered how much information and energy was surging through it, and I relished the time just to be. After a few moments, though, I had a question.

"What is going on with this spot at the top of my forehead, don Juan? All of you seem to be paying attention to it now and it was never even addressed before."

Don Juan smiled. "What is happening is that your rattle is emerging from that spot. Just keep on doing all of the variations of fire breath that you have been taught. The serpent is lengthening. A practitioner who can See will be able to discern the energy emerging from there. Remember that the serpent is your wisdom and longevity. The more you cultivate it, the more the energy will protrude. Advanced practitioners often wear head rags or scarves to hold the energy there, as it becomes quite long with age and practice. Despite what you may think, you could live to be quite old, Merlina."

I thought about his words for a moment and then shared an insight with him. "In the mythology of several ancient cultures, there was a creature called a unicorn. This being had a horn that emerged from the spot to which you are referring. It could not be touched, since the horn was the sexual and creative potential of a magical being. This horn represented purity and the unicorn could be of either male or female gender."

"Yet somehow it was both," don Juan added, although I knew he had never heard of the creature.

"Yes, don Juan. That's right. Yet somehow, it was both," I repeated.

"And did they also have stories of the luminous cocoon of man?" he asked me.

"No, don Juan. I don't believe they did." I answered him.

"That's too bad," he lamented, "for therein lies the mystery, you see. Once the rattle, the horn, or antenna starts to emerge, the luminous transformation is not far behind. Just like the cocoons of doña Celestina's moths, which you have observed with your own eyes, so is the luminous cocoon of man. Being human can become a prison riddled with worms, a dried-out hollow shell of dust, or it may be an emergence into a world of energetic transformation that is something far beyond words, wonderful, inconceivable, vastly exceeding even our wildest imaginations."

PRACTICE NINETEEN

BALANCING THE FOUR ENERGETIC COMPARTMENTS

1. Set up the Dreaming intent to ascertain the condition of your four energetic compartments. You might, for example, Dream of encountering a stove with four burners. What is the condition of each of the burners? Are any missing, disabled, covered, or clogged? What is the condition of the stove in general and of the place where it is found?

2. Attempt to cleanse your compartments. Make any repairs that are necessary. See if you can discover the location of any that are missing.

3. Attempt to activate the compartments in Dreaming. If, for example, they are the burners of a stove, see if they can be ignited. Do not force anything. Simply see which compartments will activate and which will not. Ask your energy body for discernment as to any problems you may encounter.

4. Bridge Dreaming in ritual onto your Mesa (see Mesa Practice, page 82). Clear the mesa entirely, storing your implements of sexual energy in a safe and sacred place. Accompany this clearing with recapitulation of all the sexual energies represented, and of any revelations you may have encountered in your Dreaming regarding your energetic compartments. The result should be silence and emptiness.

5. Select four candles to represent the four compartments and place them on the mesa either in the form of a Medicine Wheel (a perfect circle twice bisected by lines that divide it into four equal quarters, making the form of a cross; thus the four candles would be placed north, south, east and west) or in the shape of burners on a stove.

6. Ignite each of the four candles in the order your energy body guides you to use. This in itself will tell you a great deal. If you feel that one of the candles should not be illuminated, remove it from the mesa and place a small bowl of water filled with a few flower blossoms in its place.

7. Reenter Dreaming the next night and examine the four compartments again. Perhaps you will Dream of them as four separate and adjoining gardens. Are the gateways between the gardens open or blocked? What is the condition of each garden and what is its nature?

8. Bridge your Dreaming onto the mesa and work with the candles and water again. This time, place four bowls of water with flowers to represent the four compartments on the working area of the mesa. If any area does not feel cleansed, if the water does not respond to it, substitute the corresponding candle in its place and ignite the flame.

9. The goal is to be able to work in groups of solid fours, or in pairs of two and two, in other words at full force, and to have this mirrored by your Dreaming, which must confirm that all of the perceptions you are having in your mesa work are accurate and balanced.

NON-EARTHLY
REALMS OF ENERGY

A STRANGE MOOD OVERTOOK ALL OF US, AS IF WE KNEW that soon everyone would be going their separate ways again for a while. The next morning we all had breakfast together out on the patio and Chon announced that he had Dreamed he should be getting back to southern Mexico. Everyone nodded in silence, each one's eyes reflecting their own inner knowing. Doña Celestina thanked him for all that he had done for her clients, and invited him to return the next time he felt that it was appropriate. She told him that he was always welcome and she hoped that he would come back to San Luis again soon.

Chon asked me if I would be willing to drive him to the town of Mexicali, so that he could catch the afternoon train for Mexico City. Don Juan suggested that this would be a good opportunity for us to return to Pozo together, since Mexicali was on the way, approximately half the distance between Pozo and San Luis. I agreed, feeling a tinge of sentimentality that the three of us would be departing within a few hours.

After the decision had been made, our mood changed to that of levity and we all enjoyed second helpings of coffee and *chilaquiles,* a casserole made of shredded chicken, crumbled corn tortillas, onions, chili sauce, and cheese. The morning was cloudless with a fresh easterly breeze and the sun shone dazzling and brilliant, yet mild. Chon joked that he could probably look forward to another month of rain when he arrived in the area of San Cristobal de las Casas, which is where he would be until the spring. He said that he didn't know if the brim of his hat would endure even one more deluge and made hilarious gestures, imitating how he would look with a soggy hat and head.

We talked, laughed, and lingered at the table until necessity obliged us to attend to our own affairs. Chon and Don Juan set themselves to packing up any things they would be bringing with them. I did the same. Doña Celestina went to her consultation room and the four girls cleaned and cleared the patio area, dining table, and the kitchen. After I had finished my packing, I went to doña Celestina's altar room to say goodbye to her and thank her privately. She was not in consultation, but rather simply sitting at her altar table deep in thought, with the sun streaming through the open window.

"I wanted to thank you for everything, doña," I said to her after tapping at the open door and requesting permission to enter.

She nodded as if it all had been merely a matter of course. "Come in, Merlina. I'll see you on the Cocopa reservation in a few months," she said. "There's going to be a ceremony I'll be attending. You've done very good work here, my dear, but don't think that you're finished yet. Juan has more in store for you after the two of you get back to Pozo."

I swallowed my apprehension. "Thank you for having me in your home," I said to her sincerely. "I can't tell you how much I've learned."

"You don't have to tell me, but be sure to tell someone!" she joked, cracking a sly smile. "I still See you becoming a storyteller, Merlina." She stood up from her mesa, put her arm approvingly around my shoulder and walked me out to the passageway.

These sorcerers definitely did not stand on sentimentality or ceremony. When everyone was packed and it was time to leave, we simply exchanged words of respect and thanks once again, and left. We made our way out to my waiting jeep, carrying our things. Chon placed his belongings in the back seat beside him and don Juan and I got into the front. Within moments we were off, slowly rolling down the narrow, sandy streets of San Luis, a cloud of dust behind us.

The ride to Mexicali lasted about one hour. Chon and don Juan laughed and told stories most of the way, mainly about acquaintances of theirs that I had never met. I was glad for the opportunity just to listen and drive and not to feel it necessary to contribute anything to the discussion. Driving with either one of them could become otherworldly in a heartbeat and I needed all my attention for the road, so as not to miss crucial turns or take the wrong exits.

We arrived at the train station with time to spare. Chon unloaded his gear and sacks of desert plants. I took note of how much gear still remained in the jeep. Evidently the rest had been packed by don Juan. It seemed to be much more than we had brought with us, and looked as though someone were planning to camp for several days. There were water bottles, blankets and other items that I hadn't noticed before, since Chon's items had been placed on top of them. I considered curiously the possible reasons for hauling these things with us, but I didn't have much time to devote my attention to it, since we needed to wait in line to purchase Chon's ticket.

I got out some mineral water so that we wouldn't be thirsty during the wait, and we chatted in line for over an hour. Finally, we were able to buy Chon a ticket and could sit down on a bench in the station to await the train's departure. Once we were comfortable, Chon started rummaging through his things.

"I have something for you," he said to me. Moments later he smiled with satisfaction and pulled out his highland straw hat, decorated with long strands of multicolored ribbon. Chon presented the hat to me with satisfaction. It was a work of art, a true collector's piece, complete with a little point at the top and a horse-hair tassel in the back. "It won't stand even one more rain," he joked.

I joyously accepted the beautiful hat. It was brimming with Chon's energy and personality. Suddenly, though, I had the strangest thought. I recalled don Juan's story of the gift of blankets from the sorcerer Melquior Ángelo. I inspected the hat with a newfound interest, wondering if Chon's energy body might perhaps be hiding somewhere within it. That sent Chon and don Juan into fits of howling laughter, a ruckus so loud, in fact, that I had to desist so that they would calm down. I thanked Chon for the present.

"That's just so that I can keep an eye on you until I see you again," he said to me with a wink and a shake of his finger.

He turned to don Juan and their goodbye might have been that of lifelong friends who would see one another again in fifteen minutes around the corner. I was quite moved by their dignity and unspoken affection for each other, their casual manner and the profound trust that ran between them.

When Chon's train began to board, we were hard-pressed to put him on it. He got himself a window seat and looked as happy as could be at the prospect of his long journey. We stood on the platform watching him through the window after we'd helped him load his things aboard, and then his train pulled out of the station. It was a surreal moment filled with the portent and ultimate nature of a mysterious journey.

Don Juan said to me as we walked out of the station, "Whenever anyone I know is not with me, especially if it is someone I care for, I always See them journeying into the infinite." It was a fitting and worthy tribute and it made our departure a bit easier.

We still had more of a drive ahead of us. We were fortunate, for the afternoon was as clear and lovely as the morning had been. Don Juan settled back to enjoy the ride. We were heading south from Mexicali in the direction of Pozo, but when we reached the dirt road that would take us west toward the town, he instructed me to keep on driving south.

"We're not going directly back to my place," don Juan told me.

"Are we going to camp somewhere?" I asked, finally having an opportunity to mention all the extra gear in the back of the jeep.

"I'm going to take you to a power spot I know. We'll spend a few nights. There are things I have to show you that can only be learned at such a place," he said.

I knew that he had prepared the trip in advance and that this was what doña Celestina had referred to when she told me that don Juan had "more in store." I relaxed into the drive, knowing that don Juan would give me directions at the proper time. I was very glad that I had filled the jeep with gasoline in Mexicali, because we traveled quite a way further.

We had driven south almost all of the way to Santa Rosalia, and were nearing the middle of the Baja Peninsula, before don Juan told me to take a westerly turn into the Sierra de Guadalupe mountains. We then drove steadily into the range and took several more turn-offs before we reached a place where don Juan said it would be good to park the vehicle.

"This is painted cave territory," he told me. "Some of the most massive are near here. This area used to belong to the Cumiai Indians, but other desert groups also conducted vision and Dream quests in some of these sacred sites."

"Is that why we are in this area, don Juan?"

"Sometimes," he said, "if a practitioner builds enough energy, their capacity for transformation exceeds the limitations of the Earth, and of their age and their human body. They exceed the capacity of their own body for metamorphosis."

"What happens then?" I asked him.

Don Juan looked at me firmly, as if I already knew the answer to that question. "They rely upon the development of their energy body at the point," he said finally, after a long pause. "They move into nonhuman and non-Earthly realms. This is why I have chosen to bring you to such a place. Here we are going to See beyond the human. Treat every step you take here as not of this Earth." With that, don Juan opened the door on his side and got out.

PRACTICE TWENTY

SEEING HUMAN AND NON-HUMAN ENERGY

1. Select a spot where you can remove yourself from view and observe passersby undisturbed, such as a local square or a small park. Seat yourself, perhaps on a bench out of the way, and silence your mind. Let go of all your thoughts and descriptions of "reality."
2. Breathe deeply, expanding your abdomen on the inhale. Relax your body and your gaze. Try not to allow internal dialogue to tether your perceptions.
3. Soften your focus and view the passersby with inner silence. Do not describe them to yourself in any way. See if you can suspend the deeply embedded program that describes them to you as human beings within a human civilization. Merely gaze upon them with a soft focus, as though they were a phenomena never before seen by your eyes.
4. Suspending their description thusly, see if you can achieve a glimpse of the radiant life force that animates them. Move your gaze to other items within your visual field and compare the differences. Gaze upon other human beings, animals, plants, and trees, following the same procedure. Suspend their description. Can you perceive variations, rather than merely utilizing descriptive glosses or definitions? Also include objects in your gaze such as street lamps or fountains. Deobjectify them. How is the energy of each different? How is it the same?

5. Attempt to view everything just as energy, not as animate or inanimate. Ascertain differences not based upon preconceived concepts, but rather based upon the faculty of pure perception. Try feeling the world with your eyes. The results may surprise you. It is very renewing and beneficial to the body and the mind to relax imposed structures or consensus agreements and See in this way.

THE
DEATH DEFIER

WE HIKED ABOUT A HALF MILE FROM WHERE WE'D left the jeep, carrying blanket rolls, water gourds, and packages of dried fruits and meat tied onto our backs with thin rope. Twilight was imminent. We rounded a bend and I caught sight of our destination. It was a huge open-mouthed cave with gigantic red-and-black figures muralized on either side of the entrance and upon all of the stone surfaces surrounding it.

Don Juan asked me to go and collect firewood while he went inside the cave to prepare the fire circle. By the time I'd returned he had unpacked all our gear and placed it deep inside, underneath a large overhang. There was a place cleared for the fire, centrally located inside the cave but closer to the entrance.

"This is how things will work," he said to me as he arranged the sticks and mesquite branches I had collected in preparation for lighting the fire. "From twilight each night until dawn you will not speak or make a sound of any kind that is not necessary for your survival. Only my voice will be heard, since the spirits of this place are familiar with me. From sun up until sundown is the time to eat. No food will be consumed after twilight. During the day you may walk around, but when the sun begins to go down you are to return to this cave, no matter what." He paused and peered into my eyes to be sure that he was clearly understood.

"Each night I will build a fire on this spot and call to the energies that surround this place in my own language. You will not know what I am saying, but your energy body should understand. You will gaze into the fire, or at the figures painted within this cave until you feel sleepy. Then you will go to your place over there against the cave wall and Dream. Your intent will be to Dream and nothing more. The energies of this place will do the rest. If you return to normal waking awareness during the night, you must come back to the fire before going again into Dreaming. I will be with the fire all night.

"In the morning we will be able to talk and we will answer all of your queries. During the afternoon, I'll rest and we will repeat the process over again each night for three consecutive nights." He paused again, gazing into my eyes to check my understanding and compliance. "It is all right to leave the cave in Dreaming during the night, but only in that manner may you exit. I will be seated across the fire from you, facing you, with my back to the entrance to make sure you don't try to run."

My eyes must have doubled their size. Don Juan disregarded my apparent apprehension as he ignited a spark. He signaled to me that I should go to the bushes and attend to my bodily functions. I was grateful for the opportunity. I had learned from don Juan, while conducting other ceremonies in the desert, that restricting the intake to minimal quantities of dried meat and water consumed only during the daylight hours has a twofold purpose. It not only enhances one's ability to enter trance states and Dreaming, it also diminishes the need to relieve oneself. The absence of bodily functions is a desirable and necessary by-product, since it is often not permitted to leave the ceremonial area during the course of the night.

By the time I returned, the fire was beginning to blaze. I entered the cave in a stooped position, as don Juan had taught me to do, even though the arch of the entrance towered above my head. I had been instructed that bowing, bending, or even crawling is the appropriate form of respect to display when entering sacred womb spaces. I intended to muster all my respect and to show it to the utmost in this otherworldly vortex.

I settled into my spot and waited for don Juan to begin. As soon as it became completely dark, he started chanting. I had heard him sing before, but this did not in any way diminish its powerful effect. His voice became raspy and rattlelike as he droned the melodies over and over. The words were indistinguishable to me. The sounds were ancient and guttural, their mesmerizing effect, startling. Within moments the cathedral ceiling of the cave began to vibrate. The shadows cast by the fire leapt upon the giant figures painted inside the cave walls, huge red-and-black anthropomorphs, definitely not human. They loomed with increasing intensity until I felt my body lowering involuntarily.

I sat curled up in a ball near the fire and felt the need to crawl to my blanket. The sounds began to reverberate as I made my way on my hands and knees. When I reached my bedding, I wrapped the blanket around me like a cocoon and closed my eyes, hoping to decrease the pounding in my head. Everything began to spin. I tried opening my eyes again, but that made the whirling worse. Soon I felt the heavy weight of slumber coming upon me. The vibrating echoes were becoming almost intolerable. Shortly afterwards, I don't know how, I seem to have fallen into a deep sleep.

I awoke in my energy body without any feeling of dizziness. Don Juan was singing at the fire but the effect was minimized. It was as though the sound had been turned down. Everything seemed to be moving in slow motion. Even the flames stood still for seconds at a time. I had the strong desire to walk outside. As I passed by the fire, I could see a glint in don Juan's eyes. They were rolled up and back, beneath his slightly parted lids.

I easily made my way through the entrance and took a deep breath of the fresh night air. I looked up into the cloudless, moonless sky. Somehow it was still luminous, as though it were lit from behind. I noticed then a comet trailing across it. That was odd. I wasn't aware of any comets in the area. Then I spied a massive shadowy figure on the desert floor. At first it appeared perhaps to be a gigantic cardon cactus, but on closer inspection the figure seemed to be moving. I inched a little closer still and then I paused. Suddenly, I heard the sound of far-off thunder and that stopped me dead in my tracks.

I realized that I was not looking at a cactus. What I saw was alive and yet it did not seem to be living as we know it. The creature, whatever it was, turned and saw me standing outside the cave. I could not run. The being began to move closer. One would have expected it to lumber along on account of its size, but it gracefully avoided bushes as it passed. I was enthralled. There was a ripple effect, like a wake or a flowing cape that followed and surrounded the being. It seemed to be negotiating a large serpentlike tail, yet it moved upright on two legs. The being was easily twice my size.

The fire from the cave cast light upon it when it came close enough. I drew in a deep breath. I was gazing at a fully intelligent countenance. The eyes were burning. Its head was topped with three horns. One was positioned at the crown of the forehead and the other two were at the sides of the head, above the ears. The creature appeared to be red and black, like the gigantic figures painted on the inside walls of the cave and all around the entrance. I thought perhaps I might be Seeing the guardian of the powers of this place in Dreaming.

Then the being looked me full in the face, lowering its head to observe my eyes in the night. The features were beautiful, symmetrical, and somehow classical! I realized that this was a creature far more evolved and sophisticated than I. It was easy to observe from the face, horns, and body that this being maintained a balance between masculine and feminine, a perfect hermaphrodite, and that it was not of this world. I began to wonder if I was observing a deity of some sort. There were aspects of it that appeared almost humanlike—the face, the arms and legs and graceful torso—yet it was beyond this. The massiveness, the coloration, and the horns were definitely representing something far outside our evolutionary uses of sexual and life-force energies.

The comet sputtered overhead and luminous rainbow sparks fell everywhere from it, firing up the sky and enabling an almost daylight view of the being that stood before me. The creature did not speak but pointed instead to the trailing comet with the long index finger of its right hand. Then it reached out and touched a place inside my chest with the same finger. As it did so, I felt something explode and reconfigure within me. My eyes burned and were completely absorbed in a sensation of light.

I heard from that light another thunder clap and awakened inside my blanket roll. The light of the rising sun was inching its way through the cave opening. The fire was now just a pile of friendly smoldering ashes, and don Juan sat just as I had seen him, looking surprisingly rested and at peace, considering that he had been tending the blaze all night.

After covering the ashes with sand to make sure that they were extinguished, don Juan opened some packages of dried apricots and dates. I took one of the gourds of water and we sat outside the cave to enjoy our breakfast. The desert morning was fresh and beautiful. The early sun shone upon the smooth stone surfaces, fading them to white and lightening the color of the painted giants to shades of earthen pink and pastel gray, rather than red and black.

"These figures are an accurate representation of what I saw in Dreaming last night," I commented as I took them in for the first time in full daylight.

"They were not painted by one artist or even by one group of people, but rather by many who have come here over thousands of years and have all seen more or less the same thing," don Juan told me.

I looked at the figures directly across from us and realized that even the horned head was accurately represented from various different artistic perspectives. "What was it that I Dreamed, don Juan? At first, I thought that I might be Seeing the guardian of this place, but later I came to feel that it was something else entirely."

"That being is beyond this world and beyond this life and death," don Juan said. "It belongs somewhere outside humanity, and yet as you Saw, it has humanlike qualities and masculine and feminine energy. Remember that I told you that there are energies that exceed the human or Earthly capacity to hold them. They are transformational energies outside of this realm. Sometimes the body encounters them. That is a sign that one is headed for something beyond all this," don Juan gestured around at the environment surrounding us.

"Just as the power of your energy body may exceed the ability of your physical body to hold it, as you experienced last night in the cave when your energy body began to emerge and your physical body had to sleep, so does the energy body at times exceed the capability of the Earth to contain it within the Earthly domains. Tell me," he said, "did the being touch you in any way, anywhere at all?"

"Yes. It touched my chest, near the heart," I answered him, somewhat astonished that he knew to ask this.

"That is most significant," he said, nodding to himself. "You see, that being imparts the possibility for transformation outside of this human drama we call life and death. This requires an energy body, of course, and so you had to be able to rouse yours and meet the being on its own terms. What happened is that it planted a portion of its own energy within you, something that you will become when you emerge from your luminous cocoon."

I was speechless. "Have other peoples seen this being, don Juan, or is it something peculiar to the Seeing of desert shamans?"

"I'm not sure about peoples from other lands, though I sense that perhaps some might have seen the being in a similar or perhaps a different form," he said, taking some time to contemplate my question. "I do know that other Native cultures have seen it. The Nahua have seen it and Chon, who is Maya, has also seen it. The being is very selective, however. It seems that one must have developed the energy double in order to be given the view of it, or the opportunity to be in its presence, otherwise one will misunderstand it."

"Does it have a name?" I asked.

"To know the name of something means that you have the power to call it at will. That being would never allow such a thing. It bestows its energy, you see. I like to think of it as a being who goes beyond the energy of death by conveying the possibility of a transformation that exceeds it. That is how I See it. Perhaps you could call it the death defier."

PRACTICE TWENTY-ONE

DREAMING DEATH

1. This is a Dreaming task transmitted by the energy of the death defier as seen by desert shamans. It is used to practice for the moment of death.
2. This Dream must be allowed to occur. It cannot be forced. One enters into a state of Dreaming and allows the Dream to become that of one's own death, not in a prophetic sense but rather simply as practice. The death process may be activated in the Dream by a being outside of oneself, or one's own energy body may initiate the practice, once the practitioner has sufficient control and awareness of what is being undertaken.
3. Allow the death to occur, Dreaming your way through the process rather than becoming frightened and waking up. This second response is most common, as it is an instinctive one engendered out of fear. However, it may be overcome.
4. Allow total nothingness to occur without permitting any interruption of your Dreaming awareness. If an interruption is unavoidable, do not stay with it any longer than necessary. Become the nothingness. Then begin to reconfigure your awareness, cleansed and more essential than the prior configuration. Do not degenerate into ordinary dreams or into Dreams of ego.
5. Rather, strive to bring the essential awareness back with you into the waking world in simple, silent, empty humility. Focus upon peace.

THE EAGLE

DURING THE AFTERNOON WHILE DON JUAN was resting, I took a walk around the area. There were several trails leading to other mural sites, the most memorable of which was a stone panel covered with large, black, open-winged flying creatures that were perhaps intended to be eagles. In examining the figures it seemed that each was portraying the same thing, though the artists had deliberately avoided depicting the head of the creature and so it was impossible for me to be certain what was being represented, without don Juan's presence. Still, for some unknown reason, perhaps due to the wing span and the shape, I sensed that they all depicted the same form of eagle.

I didn't stray too far from the cave, since don Juan had given me very specific instructions about returning before twilight. On the way back I collected some fire wood and, by the time I reached the muralized cave, the sun had just set. Don Juan was preparing the fire circle as he had done the night before. Settling into my spot within the open chamber, I wondered what the night and Dreaming would hold, but I silenced these thoughts. Don Juan's instructions had been to intend Dreaming and nothing more.

Once the sky was black and the fire was burning brightly, don Juan commenced his chanting again. The words, the rhythms and the melodies were different from the previous night, but that was all I was able to discern. One of his chants included an occasional high-pitched shriek which sent chills through my body. Each cry was then accompanied by something that he cast into the fire. I could not see what this was, but whatever he cast into the fire caused it to leap up at his words.

I held on to my waking awareness longer this second night, but after a time I began to notice shadows hovering and swirling on the roof of the cave. Observing them made me extremely dizzy and the only way to stop the sensation was to lie down on my blanket and close my eyes. Once I had done so, the sounds of the fire seemed to amplify until I felt that the blaze would swallow and burn me whole. At that point, I became engulfed in warmth and began to drift off to sleep.

When I awakened into Dreaming, my energy body was on the roof of the cave looking down upon my sleeping body. From above, I could clearly see don Juan's body sitting by the fire, casting sticks into it from time to time. I could not, however, hear any singing, although his lips appeared to be moving. I scuttled across the cave ceiling like a spider and, when I reached the entrance, my energy body lowered itself on a silvery thread, sliding down gently until I was near enough to the ground to focus upon it from the perspective of my normal height.

I patted my arms with my hands. I seemed to be myself. How I had become so tiny for a moment was a mystery to me, but it had enabled me to sneak along the cave roof seemingly unnoticed and to travel above the blazing fire without being singed. Now that I was standing on the ground outside the cave, I turned back to look inside. A huge black shadow, such as those I had seen hovering above me earlier during the night, swooped down at that very moment to block the entrance so that I could hardly make out the interior features and fire within.

I recoiled when I realized that the shadow was palpable, the consistency of a dense black gas. There seemed to be one spot that was burning within the blackness. I thought to myself that I was witnessing the birth of a new galaxy. Then the spot became a huge yellow eye that was peering at me from the center of a black aquiline head. The wing span at its base became discernible and stretched into infinity. I was gazing into the center of the universe!

Somehow the universe became a black eagle and the eagle, a universe. It fluctuated over and over between these two views. Suddenly, I was burned with its singular yellow-white-hot core at a temperature I would have thought inconceivable. I was reduced to a tiny pile of golden dust. The eagle peered at the pile of dust. Its eye became so large that it encompassed my entire scope, the totality of my vision. The eagle then selected one golden speck with its beak from the pile of golden dust that I was and flew off with it, revealing the illuminated entrance to the cave as it moved off.

My awareness reconfigured as soon as the eagle had departed. Had don Juan not been within the cave, and had he not admonished me about returning to it, I might not have been interested in doing so, such is the daring boldness of my energy body. I felt a clean break from my sleeping body. Still I knew that the transformational cycle was not yet complete. Out of respect for what we were both endeavoring and becoming, I had to return.

Returning, however, was not as easy a matter as I at first might have thought. I had changed forms so many times that it was not possible to backtrack and become what I had been. In order to approach my body again, I had to give up being the little pile of gold dust and become just pure nothingness. Only in that form could I float through the cave past the fire and hover over the sleeping body that I came to reclaim as myself.

When I awakened in the morning, I saw don Juan sifting sand through his fingers onto the remaining ashes, to be sure that the fire was out. I lay in my blanket and looked up at the roof of the cave. The morning light seemed cold in comparison to the fires I had experienced in Dreaming. I rolled up more inside my blanket and turned to lie on my right side, so that I could look easily out of the mouth of the cave. Breathing the air of the new day began to revive me. The dawn could not betray the texture of what had been present during the night.

After eating some dried meat outside the cave and splashing our faces with a little water from one of the gourds, don Juan and I walked along the trail that led to the muralized, headless eagles. Having experienced the energy in Dreaming, I now understood why the heads had not been represented. We sat down with our backs against smooth boulders, so that we could talk about the past night.

"Can you give me some guidelines that can help me to understand what happened to me last night, don Juan?" I asked him, once we were seated comfortably in the mild light of the sun.

"You Saw what we See, that is all I can tell you really," he said to me. "The Eagle is a way of perceiving the scrutinizing force that tests the substance of the universe for incorruptibility. Everything is Seen by the keen eye of the Eagle. It misses nothing, no matter how seemingly small or insignificant. Normally, this force is called to test our being at the moment of our death, but a powerful shaman can call it to come earlier. This is done as a means of preparing.

"When the scrutinizing force is applied at the moment of our death, it consumes all life force and awareness that is attached to illusion. For many human beings that means everything they've got. The Eagle tests for incorruptible energy with the flames that forged creation. So whatever cannot stand up to a burn of that magnitude is vaporized, gone." He snapped his fingers.

"The Eagle will not kill, though," he continued after a dramatic interlude. "Death must come first. So if the shaman succeeds in calling the Eagle prior to physical death, by offering a shamanic death, then it is possible to See how the Eagle will treat the offering. If the offering is rejected, if the energy is corruptible, nothing will remain of the shaman's power. If, however, the offering is accepted, if something survives the flames from the eye of the Eagle, then it will take a tiny sample of that and fly off, in order to seed it somewhere else.

"That is the accord ancient shamans struck with this energy. There is very little that can endure such a test. Only gold survives a furnace that hot to emerge uninjured and pure. That is what your Dream was all about."

My fingers flew to my lips as I drew a deep breath in realization.

"You passed," don Juan said to me, looking fixedly into my eyes. "You were reduced to your essence. There was something in your awareness and life force that had the ability to stand the scrutiny. Gold yields purity under heat and pressure. You see? Congratulations."

"And yet I had to give up the gold in order to return to the cave," I told him, musing over the paradox.

"Exactly. The offer is a simple, and yet a seemingly impossible one. At death, one must give back everything that one has been given and more besides, in the form of thanks, and still have more than one started with. Only then may we pass the Eagle. It is not possible to cheat. The offer must be the real magic, and that is to be able to make something from nothing, for that something to become incorruptible, and for that incorruptible something to become incorruptibly nothing."

I was taken aback by the poetic elegance of the magical language of energy. Nothing in my life, but life itself and the love of it, could possibly have prepared me for such a simple truth. I asked don Juan if I could spend some time alone at the site to voice my thanks. He understood completely and walked back to the cave to have a rest, leaving me there alone in what was becoming a beautiful midmorning.

As he departed, he put his hand approvingly on my shoulder and then I found myself in solitude, surrounded by the muralized flights of large, headless black eagles. I wondered how many shamans before me had painted these visions upon stone in order to leave their thanks at the spot. I wondered at the encounters they might have had and at their possible triumphs or laments.

It was not really possible for me to speak my gratitude to the Eagle, to life and to Creation with words, but I was able to sing my medicine songs of thanks, songs that I had acquired through my long journeys in Dreaming and in ceremony. After I had finished singing, I noticed one solitary golden eagle soaring in the skies above. It was later joined by another, and that let me know that my prayers of thanks had been heard.

PRACTICE TWENTY-TWO

HEART OFFERING

1. There is a moving meditation which may be undertaken in part as a preparation for offering to the Eagle. It is called the Heart Offering and was practiced by the ancient Maya and Toltec. This movement is also reminiscent of the Sun Dance Offering, practiced among the Native Peoples of the Plains.

2. Expanding the abdomen on the inhale, one leans back as far as possible, expanding the arms to embrace the burning sun. The neck is completely relaxed. The head hangs back limp with the eyes open, gazing into the top of the head. The arms are limp, and yet they maintain the expanded embrace. The back is bent backwards. The legs are separated more than shoulder width apart, rooting firmly into the Earth, with the knees slightly bent.

3. Remain in this position and stretch into it fully, holding the breath within the body. Give your body over to it entirely, offering every ounce of your being and baring the heart within your chest to the blazing sun overhead.

4. Hold this position until your chest burns and you feel the heart energy center expanding with light and heat. Keep holding until you feel that you are about to lose consciousness. Visualize the Eagle taking a bite of your heart at this moment.

5. Now rise erect, bringing your arms over your head. Bow deeply, keeping the arms overhead and letting them gracefully follow you downward. Profoundly exhale as you bow down, keeping your legs straight, stretching your spine, and touching the ground with your palms. Release every bit of breath and self, until you are completely empty. Stay with the bow and exhale a little longer, contracting the abdomen all the way in on the exhale, until there is nothing left of you but pure nothingness.

6. Stand erect, inhale, and give thanks, bringing your arms to your chest and placing your palms together in a prayerful position over your heart.

7. Know that each time you offer, you purify. Concentrate on incorruptible love when you practice. Do not think of yourself. Rather be thankful that you have something to give. Give everything to the Eagle. Return everything you have received without bitterness or selfishness. Magnify what you have received by giving thanks for it, as you return your utmost all in offering.

THE FIRE
WITHIN

OUR LAST NIGHT AT THE CAVE DID NOT BEGIN LIKE the others. Don Juan had me stay at the fire circle while he went off to get the wood. Then we built the fire together. After the fire was burning, I went to my place across from him and expected him to start chanting. Instead, he pulled his river cane flute out from his blanket roll and began to play.

The haunting, longing melodies he played are forever engraved upon my memory. The entire desert became still and silent and it seemed that the chamber where we were moaned with each soft yet penetrating tone. The round notes hung like globules in the cool air, manifesting visually in front of my eyes. The effect was so overpowering that it caused my spine to relax. In order to hold up my weight, I had to lie on my back and let the waves of song wash over me. It was in this way that I drifted off.

The next thing I remember was awakening into Dreaming and seeing don Juan's face gazing into mine, just inches above me. I was startled that his face seemed so close. He told me to get up, that it was time to go. Willingly, I rose to follow him out of the entrance to the cave, past the warm, burning fire. I was not concerned that we would be leaving our physical bodies behind us.

When we reached the mouth of the cave, he turned to look at me. He was almost fully turned around facing me, when a white light flared. I lost all visual perception, except for the white light. It was as if a supernova had exploded between us. I knew he was there, and yet I could see nothing but the light.

Even though I could see nothing other than white light, I sensed there to be a shimmering river outside the mouth of the cave. Somehow it was perceivable in the texture of the light. We would need to cross it. I felt don Juan reach out to take my left hand, and together we walked across, although I could never see the water. It was only once we were on the other side that my vision returned. I could then clearly see the open cave with the silvery stream flowing in front of it.

The world where we found ourselves was not like this one, but rather a world made up of rainbows. Everything was holographic. We were luminous beyond the most exquisite vision of luminosity. I knew it was here that we would emerge from our cocoons to become this Dream that was still evolving. I felt so much love, so much energy and abundance . . . and then I awakened to find myself looking up at the roof of the cave.

It was perhaps three in the morning. Don Juan had stopped playing his flute and a night bird was singing sweetly. The fire was still burning and he sat across from it in silence. I returned to my spot there and enjoyed the warmth and the glow of the flames. I felt no need to return to sleep. In fact, I felt as though I might never need to sleep again.

When dawn came, we let the fire burn out and sifted sand upon the last smoldering ashes. Don Juan thought that it would be a good idea to leave the spot thusly, so we gave our thanks, tied our gear upon our backs and hiked back to the jeep. The sun was barely up when we got to the jeep. We both had the notion that we should drive to the coast near Santa

Rosalia and have a discussion there, amidst the translucent natural beauty that is the shoreline of the gulf.

We breakfasted lightly in the jeep along the way, and within an hour and a half we were off-road and driving up the sandy coast. In a private cove, seated near the sparkling sea, don Juan began what was to be our last lesson. "That final Dream is bridged at the moment of death," he said, looking out at the calm water glistening in the sunlight. He lay back on his elbows and put his hat down slightly over his eyes. "I'll go first, just as you Saw it. I'll be there, in that place we Dreamed, and I'll meet you there when you leave this Earth."

I contemplated his words. "Where will we be?" I asked him.

"There is no road map to get there," he said. "You must pass through the fire and cross over the spirit water, just as you Saw it in Dreaming. It is a real land, a pure land of the highest vibration. It exists before the formless infinite. Perhaps our journey will take us into infinity, once we are reunited."

"How do I get there?" I pondered, marveling at the wonders of Dreaming.

"It is a matter of the energy body," he replied gently. "No one can arrive improperly. The energy of that place is not predatory and so only the truest intent and the purest attainment can herald entry. The first part of the journey is undertaken while yet alive in the physical body, as you are doing now. Through Dreaming, practice, and right living, you fund the energy. Then you must See the place and the energy that will take you there. That is the purpose of the Dream you had. Someone who is ready to leave must show it to you.

"Once the energy body has witnessed such a place and such a transformation, it begins to evolve. The Dreaming and practices then continue throughout the life of the initiate. The next step is for the mentor to leave. That will be happening soon. When I do, I'll take a portion of your energy with me. Then begins the real journey, for a piece of your living energy will be taken across.

"In order to survive, you'll have to complete the work. When I come for that piece of energy, you will See me again in Dreaming just as you did last night, only this time, we won't both just be building a bridge and sitting together to discuss our work. When I come for you again, I'll cross that bridge of energy. Then it will be for you to prepare as I have done. I will be waiting for you on the other side and after you have lived your life and completed your preparations, you too will cross the bridge of energy."

"How will I cross it?"

"The first step begins when the body nears death," he said. "At that moment, the energy body seizes the life force from it. This is what causes the blazing flash of light that you saw. It is a fire from within. The energy body fuses with life force and starts to burn with life of its own accord, no longer needing the physical body to stoke the furnace. Dreaming teaches the energy body to operate at a higher level, and with the free energy to be found in Dreaming, the life force of the energy body may be maintained endlessly.

"The next step is to exit the physical body, once your energetic capacity has exceeded it. This is done by moving through the second barrier you saw. It appears as a field of liquid light. Native shamans have called it spirit water. This barrier can be crossed by merely stepping across it with the energy body, but one must remember to do so.

"The barrier may be crossed in two ways. The first way is to be dead. The second is to cross the energetic barrier with life force burning in the energy body. This is the option we choose. We have discovered this avenue over the millennia by working with the forces you Saw on our first two nights Dreaming at the cave."

"How does the energy body seize the life force?" I asked him.

"You have to be shown how to do it. This is why the continuity is so important. One goes first, and then another after. The ability is developed in Dreaming. Rather than just leaving enough life force within the physical body to maintain minimal respiration and heartbeat during the practice, the energy body begins to extract and concentrate life-force fuel. It then starts turning that fuel into something that burns more efficiently, by combining it with higher-order energies to be found in Dreaming, and converting the combination into a self-generating source that is compatible with the nonpredatory requirements of the realm you Saw.

"Once the fuel is ready, you might say that it is very like a pearl. The energy body will come to retrieve it from the oyster, the physical body, right before the moment of death. This exit is not akin to an ordinary death in which the energy leaks out, still requiring the physical casing to further refine and concentrate it, but no longer having that option. In this form of exit, the life force, energy body, and awareness are fully capable of emerging into a higher state of being, just as a butterfly emerges from a chrysalis. When they cross the barrier, they do not drift through it without life, but rather there is an intent to what they are doing. There is knowledge and awareness and a body to house it.

"This is a butterfly made of concentrated life force, incorruptible spirit, Dreaming awareness, and light energy, four of the most durable and valuable essences in creation. Four is the number of a stable form, and with these four the serpent emerges from its old skin with its wisdom and longevity intact, trading in its physical body for an energy body of rainbow light, blazing with life force."

"The Rainbow Serpent," I said to myself.

"Indeed," Don Juan nodded in agreement. "It takes a while to shed all the skin. Just as the Dreaming awareness may be maintained indefinitely with practice, so may the life force

within the energy body be maintained endlessly, when combined with the force of an incorruptible spirit in this manner.

"When and where is this forever, you ask? All space and
time are simultaneous, but to the physical body it seems as
though time passes. The body, because of the physical concept
of time, bridges to where the energy body already is. In truth,
we are already there. And yet, always infinite new possibilities
present themselves. Since everything is simultaneous, if you
change any one tiny detail, you change it all. The universe is
always moving and so it is forever changing, omnipresent and
simultaneous, new, yet ancient and pre-existing. And we strive
to become what we already are.

"With all the possibilities out there, some of the most
valuable things that human beings possess are their choices
and their capacity to choose. With choice, we fly on the wings
of intent, always using true Seeing to guide us. I for one am
happy with my own choices. I feel that you have chosen well.
I know that you will continue to do so and you will be of help
to others. We have come to the end of a cycle, Merlina. These
lessons are among life's greatest, the best and the last that
human life has to offer. I am filled with joy that we have been
able to share parts of the path together. We will share much
more as we emerge into what we are now becoming. Just trust
your impeccability and the silent knowledge within you, and
we'll see one another again."

No one had ever spoken to me in such a manner about
such final things and such powerful beginnings. The mystery
truly is the journey and, if made properly, it evolves all the
passion life has to give. We had gone from stillness into an
explosion of light, with the sheer force of our awareness.

"Perhaps some of the hardest things we choose to do are
the goodbyes," he said. "Even though this one is not forever,
I will spare you that. I'd like for you to go back to Yuma when
we return, and work on your book. Follow doña Celestina's

advice. Keep writing about what you have Seen, Dreamed, and learned. Continue your healing work with Chon. He is a magnificent Dreamer and has much more to teach you. One day, he too will depart and so will Celestina. There will be lessons from those moments, gifts of knowledge they'll also share with you. When that time comes, you may feel that you are alone, but you will not be. All is one within the stillness.

"Continue your practice with the most vigorous intent. Try to live to be old enough so that you may share with someone, as we have shared with you. Whenever your time comes, though, you will know it as I do now, and you will be ready."

I was moved to silence and sat gazing at the sea, holding back tears from my eyes, and yet I was not sad. Somehow I was overjoyed, as if the longing of my entire life had been given wings at that moment. I smiled softly and nodded. Don Juan left our conversation at that. He felt that it was better at cathartic moments of our lives never to say too much. Instead we swam in the warm waters of the gulf above Santa Rosalia, and we took a long walk along the beach.

The rainbow serpent, upon whose back I had ridden into the very core of my being, was going to turn on itself now and swallow its own tail. Soon the energy would lift off. I would take him to his home. He would depart it, and I would never again in this life, except in Dreaming, see my friend, my counterpart and my mentor.

EPILOGUE

AFTER OUR JOURNEY, I DID RETURN TO YUMA to write, as don Juan had suggested. I remained there for the entire winter, enjoying the warm temperatures and the desert solitude. I worked steadily each day on my manuscript, as both don Juan and doña Celestina had admonished me to do. Don Juan remained in Pozo, but told me that he might return to Yuma in the spring and would perhaps see me then, after I had finished my writing task.

I saw doña Celestina once during the winter, at a Cocopa ceremonial event, and she informed me that she had been successful in liberating her client from the abusive man who had been plaguing her and her daughter. It seems that he had simply packed up one night and vanished, after successive visits in his dreams from doña Celestina. I congratulated her and she inquired how my writing was going. I told her that it was going very well and that I hoped to have a book to show to both don Juan and herself, perhaps in the autumn of the following year.

As the spring of 1994 approached, I was nearing completion of my first manuscript and I decided to return to the Smoky Mountain foothills for a brief time to enjoy the blossoms and the green trees. While visiting there, in the land where I was born, I awoke one night into Dreaming to See don Juan staring me in the face. His eyes were just inches from mine. I felt him pull at something within me and I suddenly sat up in bed with a start. I was gasping for air and had broken into a cold sweat.

I fumbled for the light and just sat in my bed shaking, leaning against the headboard for support, until it was late enough in the morning to call the Yuma reservation. Don Juan did not have a telephone, but somehow I knew that he had returned to Yuma. I could not explain the imperative need I felt to make the call, something that I would normally never have done. I sensed that it was time for me to return to Yuma immediately.

I reached don Juan's nearest neighbor on the phone. She lived less than a quarter of a mile away and was awake and at home. She told me that she had been out on her land the day before, and had seen don Juan from that distance, walking to his favorite mesquite tree. She recounted that, as he neared it, he simply dropped, and that by the time she and her nephew had been able to run over to the spot where he lay, he was dead.

I began to shudder on the other end of the line, fully comprehending the significance of my Dream and the timing of the whole affair. Trembling and hysterical, I began to blurt out the Dream I had just experienced to don Juan's neighbor, a Kw'tsan woman of about sixty years of age, a good friend with whom he had shared mutual affection and respect.

"His Spirit touched you," she told me, drawing in a deep breath that was audible over the telephone line. "You should come right away."

By the time I arrived, his body had already been cremated in the Kw'tsan tradition. Over and over again I was told the story from both the neighbor and her nephew. On that day in April, don Juan had been walking. She had seen him seemingly open his arms to the sun overhead. He had looked up and his body had dropped on the spot. They told me that he had not even been taken to the Indian hospital in order to be pronounced dead. The doctor had come there to make the pronouncement, since this was an old and most respected traditional elder. The cremation had been open and had been done that night on the ceremonial grounds, even though this type of cremation is normally forbidden in this day and age.

I was in total shock. The only thing I could think of to do, besides weep, was to go and spend time with doña Celestina. She was waiting for me at home when I arrived and confirmed all of my perceptions, and the Dream that I had had.

"He did it just as he told you that he would," she said to me. "He came for you in Dreaming that night, as his physical body was burning."

The sheer power of the whole thing was more than I could take. I asked doña Celestina if I might remain with her for a while. She told me that I was expected to do so. I must remain in their homeland for at least one year, until the Ku'ruk took place, the second ceremonial cremation of release and recapitulation that is held for traditional elders of exceptional power and significance to the community. Only afterwards would I be free to leave. This was so, she said, because don Juan had signaled in Dreaming that some of his powers were being left to me. Doña Celestina told me that I should send for any things that I might need, for I would be there all during that waiting time.

During the course of that year and a half, from the spring of 1994 until the fall of 1995 when the Ku'ruk was held, I remained in Yuma and San Luis, taking only very brief excursions of the utmost necessity elsewhere. One trip that I occasionally undertook was to the town of Algodones on the Baja, a small Mexican town between San Luis and the city of Los Angeles, California, which was the home of Carlo Castillo. It was this town that Carlo selected for our meetings.

He was dying of cancer and had requested that I see him again and, since he was not really welcome in San Luis or in Yuma, and because I did not care for Los Angeles, we found our common ground among the shade trees of Algodones.

Over many a serenaded open air luncheon meeting in the little squares, we talked and he lamented his fate. The turn of events for him were not as he would have wished and it was evident that he would have liked to change things, had this been possible for him. I strongly felt that it was possible, but unfortunately he did not. In April of 1998, just four years after don Juan's passing, Carlo finally succumbed to his liver cancer in the privacy of his home.

I was not in shock, since I had known for a long time that this was coming and had prepared, but I was saddened by the manner of his death. Carlo had been a friend of long acquaintance. For all his instruction and for all his wealth of opportunities, he had not managed to improve his end one jot, a marked contrast to the death of don Juan. I realized that how we live and how we apply our energy truly does have an impact on everything we do and everything we are, including the way we leave this Earth. This case could not have been made more plainly or more poignantly to me, for I loved them both, each in a different way.

As for Chon, he still lives happily in southern Mexico, although revolutions are again prevalent in the area. He comes up to the border from time to time and stays with doña Celestina in her home, just as before. We continue with our Dreaming and healing work. Chon says that when it is his time to leave, he will do so Dreaming. This is his natural avenue. One day his physical body simply won't rouse itself in the morning and his energy body will go on. I hope that day is a long way off.

Doña Celestina has relocated to a Cocopa town as of the date of writing this, my second book. She is quite well and fit.

Doña Celestina says that she will not join us in the rainbow world for some time to come, since her dragonlike energy body has more to do within the fiery cauldron of the Earth. Her preparations do not include leaving this world with her energy body until later. Rather, she will be navigating her energy in order that she may become even more at one with the Earth itself. Someday, though, she will leave. Doña Celestina continues to be my greatest source of female, primordial, sexual energy wisdom.

I continue my Dreaming work and practice, just as my mentors have all advised me to do. I must admit that as a result of the deep energetic journeys we have undertaken, I have changed much more than I ever expected I would. A sobriety has come upon me, a knowledge of life and death and of the paths in between. The power of our life-force energies, of creation, and of transformation continue to reveal layer upon layer of exquisite, heightened awareness embedded within mystery. The timeless elegance of it all is awe inspiring.

Some people feel that human beings are at the end of an evolutionary cycle. Based upon what I have seen and experienced, I cannot say that this is the case. I have witnessed transformations beyond my wildest imaginings rooted in the primordial powers of our sexual and life-force energies and in heightened awareness. I have Seen with my own eyes emergence into a world of spiritualized life force and light. It has been my intent in this writing to share some of the secrets and the methods utilized by the ancient nagualist sect of shamans to continue the evolutionary paths of our sexual life-force energies and our awareness. It is my hope that people will take these practices unto themselves and work with them as the gems that they are for their own well-being and betterment, and for the betterment of humanity and human awareness as a whole.

Peace, wisdom, balance, and power are the essentials if we intend to move lovingly into realms which are beyond human. In humbly undertaking to do the work with one's own energies, one can only gain, and often in ways that are quite inconceivable. I wish you well.

About the Author

Merilyn Tunneshende teaches workshops on Nagualism, a specialized branch of shamanism which has roots in Yuman, Nahua, Mazatec, and Toltec-Mayan traditions. Since the publication of her first book, *Medicine Dream,* she has also made numerous public appearances as a lecturer and panelist focusing on the healing applications of nagualist shamanism.